THIS BOOK
belongs to

....

Melissa Forti

Live, Love, Bake

PHOTOGRAPHS
Giovanna Di Lisciandro

To my mum

Melissa Forti

Live, Love, Bake

Prestel

Munich · London · New York

My name is Melissa Forti, and I bake cakes. This is what I do, and this is how I want to present myself.

Since the beginning of my career, I have done so many things, including opening and managing my very first little bakery in Sarzana, Italy, which became a tea-room and then the inspiration for my first book, *The Italian Baker*. Much has changed since then and this is my third book, but I still consider myself someone who bakes cakes. It started like this and, hopefully, it will continue like this for many more years.

My life has been, so far, an escalation of great achievements and also disappointments, because this is what life is about. But in the true spirit of "pick yourself up, dust yourself off, start all over again" (my favourite version of this song is by jazz singer Anita O'Day), I've worked my way through this beautiful thing that it is my existence with the enthusiasm of a little girl. However, and this is where I share my truth, there's also been a great deal of sweat and tears. I recently opened Café Duse, in Copenhagen, Denmark, one of my most ambitious projects yet. I welcome every new endeavour in the humblest way and consider each of them monumental, but this one has marked my personal and professional growth like no other. As a human being, and as a woman, I feel I am at a turning point and the urge to tell my story has been growing inside me more with every day.

Those who know me, know that my baking style is simple, true, and honest. Perfection, to me, is about more than the look of a cake. For a cake to be perfect, it must wake up all our senses, but even more importantly, it must speak to our emotions. This is what I love about baking: how it makes us recall a time long gone, people we love, or places we've visited and how it treats us to a moment of delight in the present, while helping us create a new vision for the future. Baking gives me the opportunity to use flavours, scents, and textures, to express history and tradition through my eyes and to explore my past, my present, and the future ahead. With this in mind, I divided the recipes in this book into three chapters—past, present, and future, with the third chapter dedicated to all the people who have dietary issues, such as gluten intolerance, as well as those who have made a conscious decision to change their food habits. There is space for all, and all should feel part of the narrative. Inclusion and connection are what I wish for our future.

Love,

PAST

PRESENT

FUTURE

Melissa's
PAST

My first lost illusion and biggest disappointment in life was the illusion of family togetherness. I don't belong to the type of classic Italian family known around the world. No Grandmothers or Grandfathers. Two parents that separated when I was way too young and no siblings either. Well, at least none I knew about until I found out I had sisters from another mother. I was, literally, a lonely child. I am not saying this to give a sad tone to this book. On the contrary: From mud, the lotus flower grows, or so they say...

Never having a real family has always felt like my biggest weakness, so I went into survival mode and made my weakness one of my biggest assets.

When I was a little girl, I played alone in my room for hours, or even days, building fantastic worlds with my imagination. I had tea with a princess in a royal palace and dressed my dolls to go to the office where they led companies. I created and decorated rooms in my doll's house, using whatever I could find—a small tea towel became a carpet for the living room, an empty matchbox turned into a coffee table, and so on. I built a shop and stood at my imaginary market stall, selling all sorts of things, from fruit and bread to clothes and shoes. And after all that, I drew and painted for hours and hours. It's absolutely incredible what the mind can do to create a comfort zone, but above all, what really impresses me, is the ability each child has to turn an uneasy situation into strength.

Nobody knew, at the time, that all those games and imaginary worlds, were preparing me for who I was destined to become.

SOME LESSONS
I HAVE LEARNED FROM MY PAST

1. Everything is useful. You may not know where you are going, but if you keep moving, the answer will come. Don't stress too much though. When you need to stop, stay put. While you rest, your brain will continue to do the work.

2. Resilience is essential and to be resilient, you must work on yourself.

3. You can't do it all alone. Even if you think you can, well, you can't.

4. Be humble and willing to admit when you need help.

5. If something doesn't make you happy, change it.

6. Never make big decisions when you are feeling anxious, nervous, or depressed. Make them when you are feeling calm and happy.

7. Whatever it is, find something that makes you smile when you do it.

8. Being alone means being able to grow without interferences.

9. Accept change. I hate change, and the more I despise change, the more life forces me to change, so I know this one is easier said than done.

My father was a very good self-taught cook and made me the most delicious dishes. I believe I inherited a passion for cooking from him that ultimately became a true love for baking. But he left and that was that.

My mother, on the other hand, hated cooking. Apart from a few recipes, such as the yogurt sheet cake she sometimes baked (the recipe is in my first book, *The Italian Baker*), or her perfect mashed potatoes, she pretty much raised me on pasta with olive oil, soups, and frozen pizza. Don't get me wrong: As a child, I didn't mind and I was by no means a neglected girl, but this simple way of eating had an impact on my palate, as well as my curiosity for the culinary world. Although I am curious, I am not an adventurous eater. I prefer simple but properly defined flavours, and I have never been into eating unconventional food. Instead, I try to find perfection in the things I like the most.

Then there was Uncle E, who was not really my uncle but my mother's first husband, before she met my father. Uncle E.

was always a part of my life, like a fun uncle, and loved me the only way he could, but in his own way. I owe him a lot. Uncle E. never cooked, but he always encouraged me in all my adventures. He passed away three years ago, leaving a great hole in my heart.

Rome, where I was born, played a pivotal role in my life and upbringing. It's called the Eternal City, but I call it the old beautiful lady. She is a crazy lady, with a temper, but also warm, welcoming, and so beautiful. Rome makes you fall in love with her every time you visit, while also being truly hard to deal with, so you can't wait to leave. You either love Rome or hate it. There is no in between. I love her with all my heart and hate her with all my guts, but when I need to find myself again, my heart always leads me back to Rome.

I get lost quite a lot, I must admit, and this is why I long to hold on to the people and places that make me feel rooted. I was born on Isola Tiberina, an island—yes, an island—in Rome's Trastevere neighbourhood and part of the historic city centre. On that island stands the Fatebenefratelli Hospital and it is there that my life journey began.

I can honestly say that Rome raised me, a bit like the Capitoline She-wolf, the bronze sculpture found near the Capitoline Hill that depicts a mythical creature feeding Romulus and Remus, the twin founders of Rome. I was, in many ways, fed by the city's beauty, history, nature, traditions, art, and especially all the delicious local food.

Rome has dozens of incredible parks and green areas, and it was in these outdoor spaces that my childhood largely unfolded. So many spots in the city hold memories for me, and most of those memories are linked to food. The zoo near Villa Borghese, one of the largest parks in Rome, was my favourite place to go as a child. It was our custom, before entering the park, to buy peanuts to give to the monkeys, and to enjoy a freshly fried bombolone (doughnut) at the stall right in front of the zoo. The smell of doughnuts still brings me back to those days.

When I was not in school and my mother was working, I spent the day with Uncle E., who took me walking around the city all day, no matter how tired I as—he was quite a peculiar character and hated cars, so he didn't own one. I will never forget a particular episode that shaped a part of my future.

My mother wanted me to become a ballerina, at all costs. It was her dream, not mine, and because she couldn't be a ballerina, I had to fix that for her. She sent me to the National Academy of Dance, founded by Jia Ruskaja in 1940, and I studied there for 12 years. The day before I had to take the final exam to pass to a higher level, Uncle E., contrary to my mother's orders, made me walk for hours and hours on a very hot Roman summer day. I was exhausted and got a blister on the bottom of my foot, preventing me from executing the perfect grand jeté. I didn't pass the exam and I was out of the Academy. My mother was furious, but I was delighted! My uncle, on the other hand, had to deal with my mother for months! Who knows, what I would have become if I passed that exam?

Walking around parks and spending time in them, was something we did all the time, mostly because it was free! My uncle used to joke a lot and play pranks on me. We would stroll around the city centre and he would say, "If you behave, and you walk without complaining, I will take you to Via Veneto to watch beautiful people eat gelato at the cafés"! And I would reply, "But I want gelato, too"! Uncle E. would laugh and make me beg for a while, but in the end, he would buy me the biggest gelato I could hold. The pistachio at the Sant'Eustachio gelateria, near the Pantheon, was to die for!

Because I rarely played with other kids, my childhood memories are of experiences around town, eating pizza for lunch, snacks like supplì (rice croquettes) around midafternoon, and gelato for dinner. Yes, I know kids shouldn't eat gelato for dinner, but my life has never been normal! And the way Rome was "feeding me", was through hundreds of traditional delicacies that changed from district to district. In this chapter, I share some of my favourites.

As a teenager, I was rebellious, and Rome became my ally. Instead of daytime walks in the parks, bicycle rides at Villa Ada, and pony rides at Villa Glori, I was out every night, rebelling against my mother and her strictness. I made nightclubs and bars my home and Rome my partner in crime. The city smelled different at night. It was pungent and alcoholic, but also very sweet! Bakeries started work at 2 a.m., and I remember quite often stopping in the middle of the night at a bakery in Campo de' Fiori Square to eat a slice of their freshly baked pizza! Or when I was craving cakes and brioches, I would go to the Prati district to visit a bakery with no name, located in a basement—one of those places only true locals know where to find.

As a child, I wasn't taught that I could become and create anything I wanted. I had no real direction, and one could say that I was "lost" for many years. Very few people are lucky enough to be born knowing their mission in life, who they want to become when they grow up, or what job they want to do. I had no clue, and for many years I searched with no luck.

During those years, I was gathering information, having experiences, and causing some trouble, but mostly and without much luck, I was trying to find myself. I think this is something we all go through at some point. I was nervous, anxious, and eager to do something though I didn't know what yet. One thing was for sure: I had to escape the suffocating reality at home. Those were very confusing years and quite frightening for a girl with no guidance, no prospects, and no means to do much with her life. Rome had become one of those friends you shouldn't be friends with, but she always protected me from danger, and I am grateful for that. We were ok, me and Rome, until we had a falling out.

When I graduated from high school, I decided to skip university and look for a job, because I had to help at home. This is when Rome started to feel like my enemy. I did all sorts of jobs, but the city wasn't offering me real options, or at least nothing substantial. I worked as a waitress, a secretary, a shop assistant, you name it, but at the end of the day,

I felt empty and depressed. Little did I know that those were my formative years, and every single job helped me gather information and experience to build my future. At the time, I couldn't see it. I wanted more from myself and more from life. Because I'd had so little until then, I believed it was finally my moment. Rome, I thought, had betrayed me, keeping me there to see how great she was without allowing me to become great like her. Or so I thought...

I didn't come from a wealthy family, and money was always an issue, which limited my options. But I was curious, and I wanted to see the world, so I packed my things and left home to live and work around Europe, including in London, Berlin, and Amsterdam, as well as in Los

"I am GROWING UP," (...)
"I am losing my illusions, perhaps to acquire new ones."

VIRGINIA WOOLF

Angeles. Looking back, I regret not going to university, because it would have provided, among many things, more "youth time." Moving away made me grow up fast, as I had to provide for myself.

And I did. I learned to speak English fluently, worked in many different fields, and studied interior decorating, which has always been a passion of mine. I also cried a lot and suffered a lot. I went to tons of parties and felt free, but I was also lonely a lot. I didn't ask myself questions like "what am I doing?" or "where am I going?". I simply did what I had to do to survive. And although I didn't know it at the time, there was magic happening once again. Those were formative, important years, and every single thing I did, would be useful later on.

Life is a matter of choices. I took mine and they led me to where I am today. I still don't know if I made the right choices, but I know that I did what I could with what I had, and this is one of the lessons that life has taught me that I will never forget.

Like many young people spending time abroad, eventually, I went back home. My mother made me come back, because, and I quote: "It is time for you find a real job and help me here, because we are alone me and you". And so, I went back, heartbroken and lost once again, back to a city that remained the same, while I was changed, a place I could not relate to anymore. I found a "real" job working as a cabin crew assistant for an Italian airline company and then in airport ground services. I had a temporary contract, and I was helping my mother pay the mortgage, but once again, I felt confused, lost, and without direction. My days of freedom abroad were gone. I didn't want to wear a uniform and I really didn't want to get stuck in a job with no future. I knew what I didn't want but not what I actually wanted. I was a depressed mess. When my contract expired and the airline declared they wouldn't hire anyone permanently, something happened inside of me that I can now see was an epiphany.

I couldn't keep working temporary jobs. The end of my contract was a sign and I had to do something about it. But what? What did I want to do? Who did I want to become? Ah! Yes! I wanted to have my own business. Yes, but what kind? Selling what? I had no clue. I told myself that when one does not have an answer, one can take some time to figure things out but still start to move. I decided to work in a shop to learn how to manage it. First, I would acquire the knowledge and then I would act.

I was hired as a shop assistant in a store that sold natural beauty products. In a matter of a month, they made me the shop manager, giving me the opportunity to learn about orders, stocking the shop, payroll, etc. WOW!! Finally, I felt I was going somewhere! And then after a year, life came knocking at my door again, showing me that this was not my place, and it was time to change again.

Through friends, I met the person who became my partner for many years, and he was from Sarzana. I was in love, and I was happy and a little naïve, but I was not scared, because I thought I met the person I was meant to be with forever. I left my job and moved to Sarzana, a move that marked the beginning of my new life, my new future, my new destiny, and a new version of me.

I will not tell you what happened after that, because it is all written in my first book, if you wish to know more. Here, it's more important for me to share where I come from and where I was going at the time. I was starting a new chapter in the charming town of Sarzana, which is in the Liguria region, in northwest Italy, and borders with Tuscany. This is where my career began, and my life really changed. Starting this new chapter, a scary one, I looked back at Rome with resentment and disappointment. Our relationship had been bumpy, but Rome was still in my heart. A part of me never left the old beautiful lady.

In Sarzana, I was blessed to find my passion: making cakes! Through baking, I could relive my past, see places in my mind, and explore my heritage, my childhood, and all the memories I was fond of but that weren't part of my life anymore. For many years, I worked nonstop. I studied pastry and then decided to challenge myself and learn by working. I read tons of books on the subject and baked for months straight and then when I opened my first shop, my career took off. I was happy and felt accomplished.

In addition to the success of my shop, I was able to work on the most amazing projects I could wish for, including being on TV, writing my first and second books, designing and curating the afternoon tea for The Royal Academy of Arts in London, and spending a year working with top chefs in Germany. I was still working at my tearoom in Sarzana, but because I was traveling so much and couldn't always be there physically, it was suffering a little. I also started working on a particularly ambitious project, which is now Café Duse, in Copenhagen.

Around this time, life came knocking once again and things changed drastically for me—and for everyone. I don't need to explain how much we were all affected by the pandemic, but the food and restaurant world got hit hard. Like many others, I had to close my shop. I thought it could persevere, but I decided to close it, which was one of the hardest decisions of my life. If it wasn't for the pandemic, I don't think I ever would have found the courage to close, but the shop had been struggling and it was time to move on. There was so much uncertainty and fear, but being closed was also starting to produce debt, which is something we all had to tackle in the business.

At first, I didn't realise the impact this decision had on me personally. I faced it like I face every challenge: by dealing with it and not thinking about it too much. It simply had to be done. During those days, Café Duse was still in the making, although we were all scared it could fail. I was losing my shop in Italy, while opening another one in a different country. Talk about mixed feelings...

Months after I closed my shop in Sarzana, it hit me. I felt like I had lost my identity. That shop represented me and all I loved. Who was I without it? I wasn't worried about failure—I have learned there is no failure in life, only lessons to be learned. But I had lost my purpose, my direction, and most of all, my kitchen!

That was one of the lowest moments in my life and I didn't know how to get out of it. I bake. That's what I do, and without it, I felt lost. Until life came knocking once again. I've learned this is the beauty of life: its ability to flow, move, and turn everything upside down, whenever we least expect it.

Eventually, the pandemic was more under control, and we could start working on Café Duse again. What a joy!!! I dove into the project with all my heart and passion, searching for a new identity, or perhaps rediscovering myself, but all this work left me feeling confused and anxious and I didn't know why. Why did I feel this way? What was all this anxiety trying to tell me?

Something was not right. I was not well. I was also feeling pressure to post more and more on social media, in some ways just to prove I still existed professionally. I hated it. I am a baker, I write books, and I am an entrepreneur. Isn't this enough?! Social media is a tool to share and keep in touch with all the beautiful people who follow me, but it doesn't define who I am. My work defines who I am. So I rebelled and decided to focus on what makes me really happy, which is the privilege of doing my job.

Meanwhile, Café Duse was progressing. The day we opened, I was so overwhelmed that I couldn't really see what was happening. I needed time to fully metabolize and accept one of the most important lessons I had to learn. There I was, inside Café Duse, looking around and feeling like a spectator, when I was meant to be a part of the show. Everything was so new, so important, so ambitious, so beautiful, and so grand that I couldn't see myself as part of it. Then it hit me. I had to let go of who I was before, to become who I am today.

Cassola Romana

INGREDIENTS

Makes 1 (20 cm / 8 inch) cake
Makes about 8 servings

- Butter and breadcrumbs (or gluten-free breadcrumbs) for the pan
- 720 g (3 cups) sheep or cow's milk ricotta cheese
- 140 g (1 cup) raisins
- 150 g (¾ cup) granulated sugar
- Pinch of fine salt
- 5 large organic eggs
- Zest of 1 large organic lemon
- Zest of 1 organic orange
- 1 teaspoon pure vanilla extract or paste (or the seeds of 1 vanilla bean pod)
- 1 teaspoon rum
- ¼ teaspoon ground cinnamon

NOTE It is important to grease the springform pan very well or the cake will stick.

Right in the centre of Rome, opposite the Tiber Island—a real island on the river Tevere—stands "Fatebenefratelli", a famous hospital, where I was born many moons ago. This is in Trastevere, which is known for its nightlife and delicious restaurants. It's a glimpse of the real Rome, and a place you can't miss when visiting the city. There, on the other side of the river, stands the Jewish Ghetto, an area filled with sad memories of an old past, as well as a lot of traditions. Today, this is a very happy and buzzing neighbourhood, full of places where you can taste the most amazing food! Cassola is a very old Jewish recipe and for many is still unknown, but not in the Ghetto, where many bakeries still follow the traditional recipe. It is a very simple and humble cake but an unforgettable one! In Rome, we used to only eat it for Easter, but now it's available all year around. If you can, use ricotta cheese made from sheep's milk, but if you can't find it, you can also use cow's milk ricotta.

METHOD Preheat the oven to 165°C (325°F). Brush the bottom and sides of a 20 cm (8 inch) springform pan with butter then coat it with breadcrumbs.

In a fine-mesh sieve set over a bowl, drain any excess liquid from the ricotta.

Meanwhile, in a small bowl, cover the raisins with lukewarm water and let them soak for about 30 minutes. After 30 minutes, squeeze any liquid from the raisins and set them aside; discard the water.

In a large bowl, combine the drained ricotta, granulated sugar, and salt. Using a wooden spoon (if you want to do it old school–style) or an electric mixer, beat until creamy. Add the eggs, one at a time, and mix to incorporate. Add the lemon and orange zests, vanilla, rum, cinnamon, and the drained raisins and mix until fully combined. Pour the batter into the prepared pan and bake for 40 to 45 minutes, or until a wooden pick inserted in the centre comes out almost clean. Place the pan on a rack and let the cake cool completely before releasing and removing the sides of the pan.

Torta alla ricotta e visciole Romana

RICOTTA AND SOUR CHERRY ROMAN CAKE

INGREDIENTS

Makes 1 (20 cm / 8 inch) cake

Makes about 8 servings

for the pastry dough

- 385 g (2¾ cups) plain flour (all-purpose flour)
- 226 g (1 cup) unsalted butter, cold and cut into small pieces
- 160 g (¾ cup plus 1 tablespoon) granulated sugar
- 5 large organic egg yolks
- 1 teaspoon pure vanilla extract or paste (or the seeds of 1 vanilla bean pod)

for the filling

- 550 g (2¼ cups) sheep or cow's milk ricotta
- 160 g (¾ cup plus 1 tablespoon) granulated sugar
- 1 large organic egg
- 1 tablespoon amaretto liqueur
- 1½ teaspoons pure vanilla extract or paste (or the seeds of 1½ vanilla bean pods)
- 360 g (1 cup) sour cherry jam

NOTE I prefer tall cakes, but if you don't mind a shorter cake, you can bake this in a 22 cm (8¾ inch) pan.

One of the most ancient Jewish communities in the world is the one that arrived in Rome around 1 BC. When two cultures come together and share the same ground, cultural blending is inevitable. And in the case of the Jews in Rome, I say thank goodness! To this day, Roman Jewish cuisine is, by far, one of the most appreciated in Rome—and around the world. The integration is so rooted that it took me years to discover that some of the dishes I thought were strictly Roman, were in fact the result of one of the most interesting cultural marriages! And this recipe is no exception. During the Shavuot holiday, it is customary for Jews to make a lot of dishes using dairy, but the papal bull in 1555 put many restrictions on the Jewish Community, including forbidding them from selling any dairy products to Christians. As a result, bakers in the Jewish Ghetto started covering the top of their famous ricotta and sour cherry tart with a layer of pastry, allowing them to elude controls. This is why this tart is so different from the ones we know today that don't typically have pastry on top.

It is no secret that I love to use ricotta in my cakes, and in Rome, the ricotta is quite phenomenal! For this recipe, I encourage you to get the absolute best ricotta you can find.

METHOD Grease a 20 cm (8 inch) springform pan.

For the pastry dough, place the plain flour on a work surface. Add the butter and use your hands to rub it into the flour until it has a sandy texture. (Try to have cold hands while you do this, or the butter will melt.) Make a well in the centre then add the granulated sugar, eggs, and vanilla. Use your hands to combine the ingredients and create a dough. (Alternatively, combine the flour and butter in a food processor and blitz until sandy then add the sugar, eggs, and vanilla and blitz until incorporated.) Divide the dough into two pieces, wrap each in plastic wrap, and refrigerate for 1 hour.

Preheat the oven to 180°C (350°F).

For the filling, in a large bowl, combine the ricotta, granulated sugar, egg, amaretto, and vanilla. Using a rubber spatula, stir until fully combined.

When the pastry dough has chilled, on a lightly floured work surface, use a rolling pin to roll out each piece into 20 cm (8 inch) diameter round. Fit one piece of dough into the bottom and up the sides of the prepared pan. Spread the sour cherry jam evenly over the bottom and top with the ricotta mixture. Place the other pastry round over the filling and use your fingers to pinch and seal the edges. Bake for 45 to 50 minutes, or until the top is very browned. It should look almost burnt on top, which is the signature of this tart. Place the pan on a rack and let the tart cool completely before releasing and removing the sides of the pan.

Frittelle di mele

APPLE FRITTERS

INGREDIENTS

Makes 12 to 14 fritters

- 130 g (¾ cup plus 2½ tablespoons) plain flour (all-purpose flour)
- 1 tablespoon caster sugar (superfine sugar)
- 1 teaspoon baking powder
- 1 large organic egg
- 1½ tablespoons rum, preferably dark
- 1 tablespoon vegetable oil, preferably non-GMO, plus more for frying
- 120 ml (½ cup) whole milk
- Zest of 1 organic lemon
- 1 teaspoon pure vanilla extract or paste (or the seeds of 1 vanilla bean pod)
- 1 L (4 ½ cups) vegetable oil, preferably non-GMO
- Granulated sugar, for decorating
- 2 Pippin apples

Here's a recipe that brings me back to my childhood, and I suspect I'm not the only one who holds warm memories of this delicious treat! The year is 1983, and Sundays were often spent at the theme park, where stalls fried apple fritters, or doughnuts, among many other typical theme park treats. I think theme park recipes deserve a chapter of their own, because in every theme park around the world, sweets change according to the local tradition, although fried doughnuts and fritters are common just about everywhere. This recipe is very simple and perfect to make with kids, provided the frying part is done by the adults, of course. Kids love to dip the apples in the batter, so get ready for a real mess in the kitchen. Nothing builds fond memories like cooking together!

METHOD Sift the plain flour into a large bowl. Add the caster sugar, the baking powder, egg, rum, and 1 tablespoon of vegetable oil, followed by the milk. Whisk to fully combine. Add the lemon zest and vanilla and whisk to incorporate. Cover the bowl with a towel and let rest at room temperature for 40 to 45 minutes.

When the batter has rested, fill a deep, medium saucepan with vegetable oil. Place over medium heat and bring the oil to about 170°F (335°C).

Spread the granulated sugar on a plate or in a shallow bowl and set near the stove.

Meanwhile, peel the apples and remove the cores. Cut the apples into slices about 6 mm (¼ inch) thick.

When the oil has reached temperature, working in batches, dip the apple slices in the dense batter then carefully drop them in the hot oil, making sure they are fully submerged. Fry the apples, flipping as needed, until golden on both sides. Place the apple fritters on a paper towel to drain any excess oil. Repeat to fry the remaining apples, adjusting the heat as needed.

Toss each apple fritter in the granulated sugar. Enjoy warm or at room temperature. Apple fritters are best eaten the same day but are quite delicious the next day, too, making them a perfect snack for a day out.

Millefoglie

PASTRY OF A THOUSAND LAYERS

INGREDIENTS
Makes about 12 squares

For the super easy puff pastry

- 255 g (1¾ cup plus 1 tablespoon) plain flour (all-purpose flour)
- ½ teaspoon fine salt
- 280 g (1¼ cups) unsalted butter, very cold and cut into small pieces
- 230 g (8 ounces) ice water

For the cream

- 4 large organic egg yolks
- 4 teaspoons granulated sugar
- 105 g (¾ cup) plain flour (all-purpose flour)
- 600 ml (2½ cups) whole milk
- 45 g (3 tablespoons) unsalted butter
- 2 tablespoons rum or another sweet liqueur (optional)
- 240 ml (1 cup) double whipping cream (heavy cream), cold
- Icing sugar (confectioners' sugar), for decorating
- Berries, for decorating

In Rome, as well as other parts of Italy, millefoglie—or as the French call it, mille-feuille—are considered a Sunday pastry. Italians enjoy pastries sitting at cafés, while drinking espresso, but it's also traditional to buy pastries to enjoy after lunch following Sunday mass, or when invited to a friend's house, in celebration of the holy day. It is very common around Italy, but in Rome especially, to see long lines of people standing outside bakeries, waiting to buy a tray of fresh pastries, and on Sundays, there is always millefoglie!

This recipe uses a simplified version of real puff pastry, but to make it even easier, you can use frozen puff pastry. If you do make your own, a pastry blender is an essential tool.

METHOD For the super easy puff pastry, in a large bowl, combine the plain flour, salt, and butter. Using a pastry blender, cut the butter into the flour, pressing the pastry blender until a very crumbly dough forms and the butter is in small pieces. Make a well in the centre then add the ice water. Use your hands (or a fork) to combine the ingredients and create a dough. (Try to have cold hands while you do this, or the butter will melt.)

On a lightly floured work surface, pat the dough into a square. Don't worry if the dough looks dry; it will work just fine. Use a floured rolling pin to roll out the dough into a long rectangle—this doesn't need to be precise. Fold the bottom third of the rectangle over the middle of the rectangle and then fold the upper third over the middle on top of the bottom third. Rotate the dough one-quarter turn and repeat the rolling out and folding process again, adding more flour as needed. Repeat this process seven more times, then wrap the dough in plastic wrap and refrigerate it for at least 2 hours and preferably overnight.

For the cream, in a medium saucepan, combine the egg yolks and granulated sugar and whisk until pale. Add the plain flour and whisk to combine. While whisking, add the milk in a slow, steady stream, continuing to whisk until there no lumps. Place the saucepan over medium-low heat and bring to a gentle boil. Add the butter and rum, if using, turn the heat to low, and stir to incorporate.

Continue cooking, stirring constantly, until the cream is thick enough to create a film on the back of a wooden spoon. Remove from the heat and let the cream cool slightly at room temperature then refrigerate until completely cool.

Preheat the oven to 190°C (375°F).

Millefoglie can be cut in squares or rounds using a round cutter. When the puff pastry has chilled, divide it into two even pieces. Place each piece on a sheet of parchment paper and use a rolling pin to roll out each piece into a rectangular that measures about 24 x 42 cm (9½ x 16½ inches) and is about 3 mm (⅛ inch) thick. Use a fork to prick the entire surface of both sheets of puff pastry to avoid bubbles during baking. Place the sheets of puff pastry on separate baking sheets and bake for 15 minutes. Turn the oven temperature down to 170°C (335°F) and bake for 25 to 30 minutes more, or until golden. Place the baking sheets on racks and let the pastry cool completely.

In the bowl of a stand mixer fitted with the whisk attachment or in a large bowl with an electric mixer, whip the cold cream until stiff peaks form.

Using a stand mixer or handheld mixer, whip the double whipping cream until stiff peaks form.

Gently fold the whipped cream into the cooled cream mixture. Keep cold.

When the puff pastry is completely cool, carefully place one sheet on your chosen serving plate. Spread the cream evenly over the surface and top with the other sheet of puff pastry. Dust with icing sugar. Use a serrated knife to gently cut the millefoglie into squares, or leave it whole, and decorate it with berries. Millefoglie is best eaten the day it is made.

Zeppole di San Giuseppe al forno per la festa del papà

OVEN-BAKED ZEPPOLE DI SAN GIUSEPPE FOR FATHER'S DAY

INGREDIENTS
Makes 6 to 8 zeppole

For the choux pastry
- 400 g (1¾ cups) unsalted butter
- 500 ml (2 cups plus 1 tablespoon) water
- 500 g (4¼ cups) 00 flour
- 1½ teaspoons fine salt
- 5 large organic eggs

For the pastry cream
- 4 large organic egg yolks
- 75 g (⅓ cup plus 2 teaspoons) granulated sugar
- 75 g (½ cup plus 2 tablespoons) 00 flour
- 500 ml (2 cups plus 1 tablespoon) whole milk
- 1 tablespoon Strega liqueur (optional)

- Candied sour cherries, for decorating
- Icing sugar (confectioners' sugar), for dusting

NOTE If you own a stand mixer, it will help you a great deal with this recipe, but if not, the choux pastry can be made using an electric mixer.

Ah! Where do I start with this one? Let me see... Well, first of all, thank you, Naples, for having created, once again, another incredible delicacy! Rome, being only a couple of hours away, benefits from many amazing recipes from Naples. It is almost as if they originated in the Eternal City, but they did not. The first zeppole date back to 1700, but the first zeppole recipe didn't appear on paper until 1837, when Ippolito Cavalcanti, Duke of Buonvicino, included in his cooking treatise. Zeppole di San Giuseppe are made to celebrate Father's Day, March 19th, but they are so good, it is worth making them all year round.

METHOD For the choux pastry, preheat the oven to 190°C (375°C). Line a baking sheet with parchment paper. Fit a piping bag with a medium star pastry tip.

In a medium saucepan, combine the butter and water over medium heat and warm, stirring occasionally, until the butter is melted. Add the 00 flour and salt and stir vigorously with a wooden spoon. When the dough starts to come off the sides of the pot, remove it from the heat and quickly stir again. Transfer the dough to the bowl of a stand mixer fitted with the paddle attachment.

In a large glass or jar, whisk the eggs. With the mixer on low, gradually add the eggs and to mix until fully incorporated.

Transfer the choux pastry dough to the prepared piping bag and pipe large rounds of choux on the prepared baking sheet. Bake for about 1 hour, or until lightly golden. Place the baking sheet on a rack and let the choux cool completely.

For the pastry cream, in a medium bowl, combine the egg yolks and granulated sugar and whisk until combined. Add the 00 flour and whisk to incorporate.

In a medium saucepan, bring the milk and Strega, if using, to a boil over me-

→

dium-low heat. Remove the saucepan from the heat but don't turn it off.

While whisking quickly, add the hot milk mixture to the egg yolk mixture in a slow, steady stream. Once combined, pour the pastry cream back into the medium saucepan and return it to medium-low heat. Cook, whisking constantly, until thick. Pour the pastry cream into a shallow bowl and cover with plastic wrap, pressing the plastic wrap directly on the surface of the cream to prevent a skin from forming. Refrigerate for about 1 hour, or until cold.

When the pastry cream has chilled, fit a second piping bag with a medium round tip. Fill the piping bag with the cream, then press the round tip into the top of each zeppola and squeeze a generous amount of pastry cream inside, continuing to squeeze until the cream starts to come out the top then use the piping bag to pipe a swirl of cream on top. Place a candied sour cherry in the middle of the pastry cream on each zeppole, dust with icing sugar, and enjoy. Zeppole are best eaten the day they are baked, but you can store them in the fridge for a day or two—they will be a little soggy but still really good!

Crostata morbida della nonna

GRANDMA'S SOFT TART

INGREDIENTS

Makes one (22 cm / 8 inch) tart
Makes about 10 to 12 servings

- 300 g (2 cups plus 2 tablespoons) plain flour (all-purpose flour)
- 160 g (½ cup plus 3 tablespoons) unsalted butter, cold and cut into small pieces
- 130 g (⅔ cup) granulated sugar
- 2 large organic egg yolks
- Zest of 1 organic lemon
- 1½ teaspoons baking powder
- 1 teaspoon pure vanilla extract or paste (or the seeds of 1 vanilla bean pod)
- Pinch of fine salt
- 340 g (¾ cup plus 2 tablespoons) your favourite jam

It is commonly believed that grandmothers know best, particularly when it comes to food, but I'm not sure this is true. I never met my grandmothers—or grandfathers—and I don't know if they were good cooks. I observed, over the years, my friends' grandmothers and I must admit that most of them were incredibly good cooks! But what I believe this idea really means is that grandmothers have always been seen as the heart of the kitchen, the keeper of the kitchen's secrets, and the one person who can feed the entire family, especially during wars and poverty, and still create magic, even with very limited resources. Cooking isn't only for surviving but is an act of pure love, and grandmothers are the epitome of love . . . or so they say.

Most grandmothers are not accustomed to using stand mixers or other modern kitchen appliances, so this recipe has you use your hands like they would. There's no special technique required—simply work the ingredients with your hands until a dough forms.

METHOD Place the plain flour on a work surface and make a well in the centre. Add the butter, granulated sugar, egg yolks, lemon zest, baking powder, vanilla, and salt. Use your hands to combine the ingredients. (Try to have cold hands while you do this, or the butter will melt.) Wrap the dough in plastic wrap and refrigerate it for at least 40 minutes.

Preheat the oven to 180°C (350°F). Butter and flour a 22 cm (8 inch) round tart pan.

When the pastry dough has chilled, on a lightly floured work surface, use a rolling pin to roll out the dough into a roughly 3 mm (⅛ inch) thick round. Fit the dough inside the prepared pan, removing any excess hanging off the sides. Gather the excess dough into a ball then roll it to the same thickness and cut it into strips for decorating the tart. Spread the jam evenly in the pastry shell. Arrange the strips of dough in a crisscross pattern on top of the jam. Bake for about 30 minutes, or until the pastry is golden. Place the pan on a rack and let the crostata cool completely. You have made a real grandmother's crostata!

Pizzette rosse Romane

ROMAN COCKTAIL-STYLE MINI PIZZAS

TA DA!!! You didn't expect this one, eh? A savoury recipe!! No, I have not gone mad. A chapter about my past would be incomplete without this recipe. It simply MUST be included! If I close my eyes, I can still smell the freshly baked pizzas my mum used to buy at the bakery near my elementary school. Every morning, a long line of cars parked in front of the bakery and while us kids waited in the car, our parents queued up to buy pizza for our morning break at school. I remember everyone running all over the place—they were late for work or school—and the traffic jam created by all the parked cars. My mum would buy pizza for me, still piping hot, and storm into the car, screaming, "Let's hurry! I'm late for work!! Can you walk to school by yourself from here"? And I would say, "But it is so cold, mum"! And she would roll her eyes and scream, "Arghhhh"!!!! Once at school, we wrote our names on the paper wrapped around the pizza and placed it on the heater to keep warm—it really was cold! I bet many of you Italian readers can relate to this. Those were the days...those were the 80's, the best time to be a kid.

This type of pizza is far from what you might think. The dough is a bakery-style dough, closer to bread than the pizza at a pizzeria, and topped with only tomato sauce—no cheese, no meat, and no vegetables. The pizzas are so greasy that the paper used to wrap them in literally drips oil everywhere! Traditionally, these pizzas are baked plain, but if you wish to add fresh mozzarella, make sure you drain any excess water to avoid too much liquid during baking.

INGREDIENTS

Makes 25 to 30 mini pizzas (4 cm / 1½ inch) or 12 medium pizzas (10 cm / 4 inch)

- 6 g (⅕ ounce) fresh yeast
- 300 ml (1¼ cups) room temperature water
- 1 teaspoon granulated sugar
- 500 g (3½ cups plus 1 tablespoon) bread flour (or Manitoba flour)
- 2½ tablespoons extra-virgin olive oil, plus more for drizzling
- 2 teaspoons fine salt
- 500 ml (2 cups plus 1 tablespoon) puréed tomato
- Dried oregano (or basil if you don't like oregano)

NOTE You can use a smaller or larger round pastry cutter to cut the pizzas, but you will need to adjust the baking time.

METHOD In a small bowl, use your fingers to crumble the fresh yeast then add the water and granulated sugar and stir to combine. Cover and let rest at room temperature for 10 minutes.

In a large bowl, combine the bread flour and the yeast mixture. Use your hands to mix the ingredients until fully combined. Add the olive oil and knead the dough in the bowl until it is elastic and mostly smooth.

Place the dough on a lightly floured work surface and knead it by pressing and rotating it for 4 to 6 minutes, or until completely smooth. Place the dough back in the large bowl, cover it with a towel or plastic wrap, and let it rest at room temperature for about 1 hour, or until doubled in size.

Once the dough has doubled in size, place it on a lightly floured work surface. Use a rolling pin to roll out the dough until about 8.5 mm (⅓ inch) thick.

Preheat the oven to 200°C (400°F). Line one or more baking sheets with parchment paper.

Using a 4 cm (1½ inch) round pastry cutter, cut the dough into circles then arrange the mini pizzas on the prepared baking sheet.

Meanwhile, in a medium bowl, stir together the puréed tomatoes and oregano, along with a drizzle of olive oil and a pinch of salt. Pour about a tablespoon of the tomato mixture on each round of dough and bake for about 15 minutes, or until the edges are slightly golden. Enjoy right away.

Bomboloni

FRIED DOUGHNUTS

METHOD In the bowl of stand mixer fitted with the bread hook attachment, combine the bread flour, 00 flour, butter, granulated sugar, eggs, vanilla, and about three-quarters of the water. Mix on low until well combined. The machine will struggle a bit but don't worry; keep going. With the mixer still on low, add the yeast and a little more water (not all of it), followed by the salt and the remaining water and knead until the dough looks smooth and dry and doesn't stick to the sides of the bowl.

On a lightly floured work surface, gently knead the dough for about 1 minute, or until smooth. Place the dough in a large bowl, cover it with plastic wrap, and refrigerate it overnight.

Line a baking sheet with parchment paper. Spread about 300 g (1½ cups) of granulated on a plate or in a shallow bowl.

The next day, on a lightly floured work surface, use a rolling pin to roll out the dough until about 6 mm (¼ inch) thick. Using a 6 to 8 cm (2½ to 3¼ inch) round pastry cutter, cut the dough into circles the bomboloni on the prepared baking sheet. Cover with plastic wrap and let rise at room temperature for about 1 hour, or until doubled in size.

When the bomboloni have doubled in size, pour the vegetable oil into a large deep saucepan. Place over medium heat and bring the oil to about 170 °C (335°F). If you have a deep-fry thermometer, now is the time to use it, but if you don't, wait for the oil to start sizzling.

When the oil has reached temperature, working in batches, carefully drop the bomboloni into the hot oil, making sure they are fully submerged. Fry the bomboloni, flipping as needed, for about 4 minutes, or until golden on both sides. Place the bomboloni on a paper towel to drain any excess oil then immediately toss them in the sugar—this must be done when the bomboloni are piping hot, or the sugar will not stick. Repeat to fry the remaining bomboloni, adjusting the heat as needed. Enjoy right away!

INGREDIENTS
Makes about 8 bomboloni

- 700 g (5 cups) bread flour (or Manitoba flour)
- 300 g (2½ cups plus 1 tablespoon) 00 flour
- 200 g (¾ cup plus 2 tablespoons) unsalted butter, at room temperature but not too soft
- 180 g (¾ cup plus 2 tablespoons) granulated sugar, plus more for tossing
- 200 g (7 ounces) organic eggs (about 4 large eggs)
- 1 teaspoon pure vanilla extract or paste (or the seeds of 1 vanilla bean pod)
- 285 to 300 g (10 to 10½ ounces) room temperature water
- 20 g (¾ ounce) fresh yeast (fresh brewer's yeast)
- 2½ teaspoons fine salt
- 1 L (4 ½ cups) vegetable oil, preferably non-GMO

NOTE As with doughnuts from many countries, bomboloni can be eaten plain or filled with pastry cream, chocolate cream, or jam. Choose what you like the most.

Bomboloni are traditionally fried, and this is what makes them so incredibly good! After all, anything fried is good. Don't you agree? I usually never fry at home, mostly because it is tricky to recycle the oil, but for this recipe, I make an exception. Please always look for the right way to recycle used oil; it's crucial for the environment.

Sugoli

STRAWBERRY GRAPE PUDDING

From Veneto, a region in northern Italy, I present sugoli, a recipe I didn't discover until I went to Venezia, and a friend made it for me. When I researched the story behind sugoli, I found out that it was primarily made during the harvest season with leftover grape must. I also learned that in the 1500s, Leonardo Fioravanti, a well-established doctor at the time, wrote about an ointment made with black grape must that was used to treat the skin of patients effected by the plague.

Sugoli is traditionally made with strawberry grapes, which are black grapes and tend to be sweeter than other varieties. Very little, if any, sugar is usually needed, but sometimes adding a little extra sweetness is required. If you can't find strawberry grapes, you can use white grapes instead.

INGREDIENTS

Makes about 4 servings

- 1.1 kg strawberry grapes on the stem
- 2 tablespoons plus 2 teaspoons granulated sugar
- 70 g (½ cup) plain flour (all-purpose flour)

METHOD Remove the grapes from the stems and wash and dry them with a towel.

In a medium saucepan, combine the grapes and granulated sugar over medium heat and cook, squeezing the grapes occasionally, for about 20 minutes, or until the mixture looks like jam. Remove from the heat and let cool at room temperature.

When the grape mixture is cool, pour it through a fine-mesh sieve to remove the grape skins or use an immersion blender and purée until smooth. (I'm not particularly bothered by the skin and use an immersion blender, so I can keep all the grapes' nutrients.) Transfer to a clean medium saucepan.

In a small bowl, combine the plain flour and 1 to 2 tablespoons of room temperature water and stir until the flour is dissolved; try to avoid creating lumps.

Add the flour mixture to the grape mixture then place over medium heat and cook for 15 to 20 minutes, or until thick. Pour the pudding into your chosen serving pots and let cool at room temperature for 1 hour then cover and refrigerate overnight. Sugoli can be made up to 2 days in advance.

Nel quale si tratta che cosa sia la peste,& da chi pro-
cede, & quello che doueriano fare i Prencipi per
conseruar i suoi popoli da essa, & vltimamente, si
mostrano mirabili secreti da curarla, cosa non mai
piu scritta da niuno in questo modo.
CON PRIVILEGIO.

Risolatte

RICE PUDDING

INGREDIENTS
Makes about 4 servings

- 1 L (4½ cups) whole milk, plus more as needed
- 1 organic lemon or orange
- 1 teaspoon pure vanilla extract or paste (or the seeds of 1 vanilla bean pod)
- 100 g (½ cup) granulated sugar
- Pinch of fine salt
- 350 g (1¼ cups plus 2 tablespoons) Carnaroli rice
- Ground cinnamon, for dusting if using lemon or unsweetened cocoa powder, for dusting if using orange

Rice pudding is one of my favourite comfort foods of all time, and I know I am not the only one. It's interesting and also quite magical to learn about the origins of this beloved recipe. In Italy, the first rice pudding recipes appeared in the Veneto region, and it was often prepared when someone was ill. Rice pudding is called Kheer in India, and it is quite popular among those who follow an Ayurvedic diet. In the UK, the first rice pudding recipes date back to the Tudor period, but we can also find traces of different versions as far away as China, Persia, and later Spain and Portugal. In some places, cinnamon is added, while in others, nutmeg and cream are used. I add a hint of citrus for extra freshness, but feel free to skip the citrus and just add a little cinnamon or cocoa. If using cocoa, you can also add some chopped chocolate or chocolate chips to make it more decadent.

METHOD In a medium pot, warm the milk over medium-low heat. Using a knife, remove the peel from the lemon or orange, trying to cut the entire peel off in one long strip (it will be easier to remove later); reserve the lemon or orange for another use. Add the peel to the milk, along with the vanilla, granulated sugar, and salt and stir to incorporate. Bring to a gentle simmer, stirring occasionally to completely dissolve the sugar. Add the Carnaroli rice, turn the heat to low, and cook, adding additional warm milk as needed if the mixture is dry, for about 30 minutes, or until the rice is creamy and properly cooked. Remove and discard the lemon or orange peel then fill 4 ramekins or bowls with the rice pudding. Dust cinnamon over the lemon version or cocoa over the orange version. Enjoy warm or at room temperature. Rice pudding can be made up to a day in advance.

Maritozzi Romani

ROMAN MARITOZZI

INGREDIENTS

Makes 4 to 6 maritozzi

- 370 g (2½ cups plus
  2 tablespoons) bread flour
  (or Manitoba flour)
- 125 g (1 cup plus
  1 tablespoon) 00 flour
- 90 g (6 tablespoons)
  granulated sugar
- 100 g (3½ ounces) organic
  eggs (about 2 large eggs)
- 140 ml (½ cup plus
  4 teaspoons) room
  temperature water
- 100 g (7 tablespoons)
  unsalted butter, at room
  temperature and cut into
  small pieces
- 12 g (²/₅ ounce) fresh yeast
  (fresh brewer's yeast)
- 2 teaspoons fine salt
- 1 teaspoon pure vanilla
  paste (or the seeds
  of 1 vanilla bean pod)
- 1 teaspoon grated organic
  lemon zest
- 475 ml (2 cups) double
  whipping cream
  (heavy cream), cold
- Icing sugar (confectioners'
  sugar), for serving

NOTE I strongly recommend using a stand mixer for this recipe—it will make your life way easier—but you can achieve good results making the dough by hand.

I recently read an article declaring Rome the best place to eat in the world. This isn't hard to believe, and maritozzi are proof! These cream-filled brioche buns date back to the Roman Empire, when wives prepared a sort of "sweet sandwich" with raisins and candied orange peel for their husbands. The best maritozzi story I found came from an old book about ancient Roman traditions by the poet Giggi Zanazzo, who explained the origin of the name. Marito means "husband" in Italian, and it was customary for young men to hide a ring in the creamy maritozzi filling to propose marriage on the first Friday in March. In Rome, there is a great deal of competition among bakeries to make the best maritozzi. It is a question of pride for Romans. There are some well-established bakeries that have baked maritozzi for more than half a century, but there is also a very interesting wave of new bakeries making maritozzi with many different flavour combinations. I wonder though: Why change something that is already perfect??

METHOD In the bowl of a stand mixer fitted with the dough hook attachment, combine the bread flour, 00 flour, granulated sugar, eggs, and about half of the water. Mix on low until the ingredients are fully incorporated. Once the first half of the water is fully absorbed, gradually add the rest. Don't allow the dough to dry out too much or the maritozzi will be hard and dry. Add the butter and mix on low until it is completely absorbed into the dough. With the mixer still on low, crumble the yeast into the dough then add the salt, lemon zest, and vanilla. Turn the mixer to medium and continue working the dough until smooth and elastic. Transfer the dough to a large bowl, cover it with plastic wrap, and refrigerate overnight.

The next day, on a lightly floured work surface, gently knead the dough for just a few minutes. Using a knife or dough scraper, cut the dough into twelve equal pieces, each about 90 g (3¼ ounces). Gather each piece into a ball using your hands then cover it with a towel and let it rest for 10 minutes.

→

After 10 minutes, line a baking sheet with parchment paper.

Use your hands to quickly roll each ball into an oblong shape—it's important to work quickly, so the dough doesn't stand in the open for too long. Place the maritozzi on the prepared baking sheet, cover with plastic wrap, and let rise at room temperature for about 1 hour, or until doubled in size. (At this point, the maritozzi can be wrapped in plastic wrap and frozen for up to 1 month; defrost them in the fridge overnight before baking).

When the dough is almost ready, preheat the oven to 180°C (350°F).

Bake the maritozzi for about 20 minutes, or until golden. Place the baking sheet on a rack and let the maritozzi cool at room temperature.

While the maritozzi are cooling, in the bowl of a stand mixer fitted with the whisk attachment or in a large bowl with a handheld mixer, whip the double whipping cream until medium to stiff peaks form.

Using a serrated knife, cut a slit from side to side in each maritozzi, being careful not to cut all the way through to the other side. Fill each with a generous dollop of whipped cream and wipe off any excess. Dust with icing sugar and enjoy right away. Maritozzi are best the day they are baked and filled.

Frappe al forno

OVEN-BAKED FRAPPE

INGREDIENTS

Makes 10 to 15 frappe

- 2 tablespoons plus 1 teaspoon granulated sugar
- 30 g (¼ cup) 00 flour
- 30 g (2 tablespoons) unsalted butter, melted and cooled
- 80 ml (⅓ cup) dry white wine
- 1 large organic egg
- Zest of 1 organic lemon
- 1 teaspoon baking powder
- Icing sugar (confectioners' sugar), for dusting

Carnival, which takes place each February, is a very beloved festivity in Italy, but I, unfortunately, am not a fan. When I was a child, carnival was always a hard time for me. At school, there was a lot of pressure around what costume to wear, and I hated it. My mother kept trying to dress me up, and I kept faking the flu, hoping I could stay home. But it never worked. Somewhere, I must have a picture of me at school, dressed as the Blue Fairy from Pinocchio and sporting the saddest face a kid can master. For me, the only good thing about carnival was, of course, the food! During this time, Italy bursts with colourful desserts from every region, but Frappe are my favourites! Traditionally, they are fried, but I like them baked, with a ton of icing sugar! In my book, frappe are the best part of carnival.

METHOD In the bowl of a stand mixer fitted with the paddle attachment or in a large bowl if mixing by hand, combine the granulated sugar, 00 flour, butter, wine, egg, lemon zest, and baking powder. Mix on low to combine the ingredients then increase the speed to medium and mix until a smooth dough forms. Gather the dough into a ball, wrap it in plastic wrap, and let it rest at room temperature for 30 minutes.

Line a baking sheet with parchment paper.

When the dough has rested, divide it into two equal pieces. On a lightly floured work surface, use a rolling pin to roll out each piece of dough until very thin, about 6 mm (¼ inch). Using a pasta cutter, cut the dough into rectangles measuring 10 x 5 cm (4 x 2 inches) and lay them on the prepared baking sheet. Refrigerate for 30 minutes to stiffen the dough. (At this point, the frappe can be wrapped in plastic wrap and frozen for up to 2 months; they can be baked straight from the freezer, but the bake time will be slightly longer.)

Preheat the oven to 190°C (375°F).

When the frappe have chilled, bake them for about 7 minutes, or until just lightly golden—frappe should be crunchy but still pale in colour. Dust with icing sugar and serve right away. Frappe can be stored in an airtight container at room temperature for up to 5 days.

Ventagli

INGREDIENTS
Makes 6 to 8 large ventagli

- 270 g (1¾ cup plus
  2 tablespoons) plain flour
  (all-purpose flour)
- Pinch of fine salt
- 256 g (1 cup plus
  2 tablespoons)
  salted butter, cold
  and cut into small pieces
- 120 ml (½ cup) ice water
- About 300 g (1½ cups)
  granulated sugar

Ventagli or palmiers? Italian or French? Who knows, but really, who cares!?! I'm just glad they exist! Ventagli used to be my go-to afternoon treat and the bigger the pastry, the better. This is why I present you my favourite version: large ventagli! It's a lot of butter and a lot of sugar.... SHHH!!! Don't think about it—just enjoy! We only live once!

METHOD In the bowl of a food processor, combine the plain flour, salt, and about half of the butter. Pulse until the butter is absorbed, but don't let the machine run too long, or the blade will melt the butter. Add the rest of the butter and pulse again until incorporated. Add the ice water and let the processor run just until a dough forms, being careful to not overwork the dough. Don't worry if the dough is still crumbly—it will come together.

On a lightly floured work surface, gently knead the dough, preferably with cold hands, until combined. Use a rolling pin to roll out the dough into a rectangle that measures 40.5 x 30.5 cm (16 x 12 inches) and is about 6 mm (¼ inch) thick or slightly thicker. Fold the rectangle lengthwise in half and then in half again. Fold it in half one more time. Wrap the dough in plastic wrap and refrigerate it for at least 2 hours.

When the dough has chilled, dust a clean work surface with a generous amount of granulated sugar. Place the rectangle of dough vertically on top of the sugar, with one of the shorter sides closest to you. Roll out the dough into a rectangle that measures 40.5 x 30.5 cm (16 x 12 inches) and is about 13 mm (½ inch) 6 mm (¼ inch) thick.

→

Next, shape the ventagli: Sprinkle the top of the dough with more sugar and use the rolling pin to press it into the dough so it sticks. Fold over about one-quarter of the dough from the top edge and then sprinkle more sugar on the folded over strip. Repeat with the bottom edge. Repeat this step and then fold two times from the top edge and two times from the bottom edge so the sections meet equally in the centre. Every time you fold a section, add more sugar. Finally, fold one side over the other. Refrigerate the dough for 30 minutes.

Preheat the oven to 180°C (350°F). Line a baking sheet with parchment paper.

When the dough has chilled, dust the work surface with more sugar and place the dough horizontally on top of the sugar, with one of the long sides closest to you. Using a long knife, cut the dough into slices about 8.5 mm (⅓ inch) thick. Place the slices at least 5 cm (2 inches) apart on the prepared baking sheet to allow room for spreading and bake for about 20 minutes, or until golden and nicely caramelized. Place the baking sheet on a rack and let the ventagli cool at room temperature. Ventagli can be stored in an airtight container in the refrigerator for a few days.

Babka al cioccolato

CHOCOLATE BABKA

INGREDIENTS

**Makes 1 babka
(23 x 13 cm / 9 x 5 inch)**

For the simple syrup

· 100 g (½ cup)
  granulated sugar
· 100 ml (6 tablespoons
  plus 2 teaspoon) water

For the dough

· 750 g (6 cups) bread flour
  (or Manitoba flour)
· 2 teaspoons fine salt
· 330 ml (1¼ cups plus
  2 tablespoons) whole milk,
  warm (about 40°C / 105°F)
· 3 medium organic eggs
· 70 g (⅓ cup plus 1 teaspoon)
  granulated sugar
· 5 teaspoons instant yeast
· 1 teaspoon pure vanilla
  extract or paste (or the
  seeds of 1 vanilla bean pod)
· 130 g (½ cup plus
  1 tablespoon) unsalted
  butter, at room temperature
  and cut into small pieces

For the filling

· 500 g (17½ ounces) dark
  chocolate, preferably 60%
  cacao, chopped
· 113 g (½ cup)
  unsalted butter
· 120 ml (½ cup) double
  whipping cream
  (heavy cream)
· 50 g (6 tablespoons) icing
  sugar (confectioners' sugar)
· 25 g (⅓ cup) unsweetened
  cocoa powder
· 1½ teaspoons
  ground cinnamon

For the glaze

· 1 large organic egg
· 2 ½ tablespoons water

A cross between bread, brioche, and cake, babka is probably the most iconic Jewish sweet. This version laced with chocolate, isn't the original, but it's one of the most popular today. Babka was first made around 1800, by Jewish women from Eastern Europe, who combined scraps of dough from making challah bread with nuts and poppy seeds. Chocolate was expensive and would never have been used in the recipe. It's believed that Jewish immigrants in the United States were the first to add chocolate, but it's now beloved all over the world.

METHOD For the simple syrup, in a small pan over medium heat, combine the granulated sugar and water. Heat until the sugar is completely dissolved then remove it from the heat and let it cool at room temperature.

For the dough, in a large bowl, combine the bread flour and salt.

In the bowl of a stand mixer fitted with the bread hook attachment, combine the warm milk, eggs, granulated sugar, yeast, and vanilla. Stir by hand with a whisk to combine the ingredients. Add the flour mixture then knead on low for about 5 minutes. With the mixer on low, gradually add the butter, little by little, to make sure it gets completely absorbed by the dough. Once all the butter is added, continue kneading on low for 4 minutes more, or until all the butter is completely incorporated. Don't worry if the dough is sticky and don't add extra flour, or your brioche will become too dry.

Transfer the dough to a lightly greased large bowl, cover it with plastic wrap, and let it rise at room temperature for about 1 hour or preferably in the refrigerator overnight.

When the dough has rested, on a clean work surface, gently shape it into a ball, without a lot of kneading—you don't want the gluten to develop too much. Place the ball of dough back in the lightly greased bowl, cover it with plastic wrap, and let it rest at room temperature while you make the filling.

For the filling, in a medium saucepan over low heat, combine the chocolate,

→

butter, and double whipping cream and warm until the butter is completely melted. Add the icing sugar, cocoa powder, and cinnamon and stir until smooth. Remove from the heat and let cool at room temperature.

Next, shape the babka: Grease a 23 x 13 cm (9 x 5 inch) loaf pan then line it with parchment paper.

On a lightly floured work surface, use a rolling pin to roll out the dough into a rectangle that measures about 40.5 x 30.5 cm (16 x 12 inches) and is a little less than 6 mm (¼ inch) thick. Once the filling is cool enough to work with, spread it evenly over the entire surface of the dough. Starting from one of the short sides, roll the dough around the filling into a log. Pinch the open edges closed to prevent spreading during baking. Refrigerate the dough for 20 minutes or freeze it for 10 minutes.

When the dough has chilled, arrange the log vertically on a clean work surface so that one of the short ends is in front of you. Using a sharp knife, cut the log lengthways in half. Gently press the halves down, so that the cut sides are facing up then braid the two halves together. Pinch the ends closed to seal them. Carefully lift the dough and place it the prepared loaf pan, cover it with plastic wrap, and let it rest at room temperature for 1 hour. (At this point, the babka can be wrapped in plastic wrap and frozen for about 1 month; let it thaw in the fridge before baking.)

Preheat the oven to 180°C (350°F).

For the glaze, in a small bowl, whisk the egg and water. Lightly brush the glaze over the surface of the babka and bake for 40 to 45 minutes, or until golden on the top. Place the pan on a rack and white the babka is still hot, brush it with the simple syrup. Babka can be stored in an airtight container at room temperature for up to 5 days.

Profiteroles

INGREDIENTS

Makes 35 to 40 Bignè (puffs)

For the choux pastry
- 125 ml (½ cup plus 1 teaspoon) whole milk
- 125 ml (½ cup plus 1 teaspoon) water
- 100 g (7 tablespoons) unsalted butter, cut into small pieces
- ½ teaspoon granulated sugar
- Pinch of fine salt
- 150 g (1¼ cups) 00 flour
- 255 g (9 ounces) organic eggs (about 5 medium eggs)
- Icing sugar (confectioners' sugar), for dusting

For the pastry cream
- 2 large organic egg yolks
- 65 g (⅓ cup) granulated sugar
- 2½ tablespoons cornstarch, preferably organic
- 1 pinch of salt
- 500 ml (2 cups plus 1 tablespoon) whole milk
- 1 teaspoon pure vanilla extract or paste (or the seeds of 1 vanilla bean pod)

For the prenz (chocolate glaze)
- 250 g (1¼ cups) granulated sugar
- 180 g (2¼ cups) unsweetened cocoa powder
- 300 ml (1¼ cups) whole milk

- 1 L (4½ cups) double whipping cream (heavy cream), for assembly and decoration

NOTE If you wish to make individual portions, you will need 4 Bignè for each serving. The decorating process is the same as for the pyramid, but you should use a small star piping tip.

Profiteroles are a truly vintage recipe in the Italian pastry repertoire. In the eighties, they were the fancy dessert to serve at the end of elegant dinner parties. Generally, the higher the better when it comes to profiteroles, but you can also find smaller versions in pastry shops around Italy. Here, I present two ways of making profiteroles. You can make a tall pyramid, or you can divide the puffs into individual portions, like I did. It's your choice. I strongly believe that great recipes are never out of date and should be kept alive. And profiteroles definitely shouldn't be forgotten.

METHOD For the choux pastry, preheat the oven to 200°C (400°F). Line a baking sheet with parchment paper. Fit a piping bag with a medium round pastry tip (I use an Ateco 806, but you can use any medium round or star tip).

In a medium pan, bring the milk, water, butter, granulated sugar, and salt to a boil. Remove from the heat. Using a wooden spoon, quickly stir in the 00 flour. Place the pan over low heat and cook, stirring constantly, for about 1 minute, or until you notice a film forming on the bottom of the pan and the back of the wooden spoon. Transfer the mixture to the bowl of a stand mixer fitted with the paddle attachment and let cool slightly.

In a medium jug or bowl, briefly whisk the eggs.

With the mixer on low, gradually add the eggs in stages. Continue mixing on low until the eggs are fully incorporated. The dough should have a thick and creamy texture, perfect for piping, and the bowl should feel warm but not too hot to the touch.

→

→

Transfer the dough to the prepared piping bag. Pipe medium sized Bignè onto the prepared baking sheet, leaving a little space between each. Dust the Bignè with a little icing sugar and bake for 5 minutes. Lower the oven temperature to 180°C (350°F) and continue baking for 30 minutes more, or until lightly golden on top. Leave the Bignè in the oven with the door slightly open to dry out for about 10 minutes. Place the baking sheet on a rack and let the Bignè cool at room temperature.

For the pastry cream, in a medium bowl, combine the egg yolks, granulated sugar, cornstarch, and salt and whisk until pale.

In a large saucepan, bring the milk and vanilla to a gentle boil over medium heat. Temper the egg mixture by slowly pouring a little milk into the bowl and whisking quickly. Pour the egg mixture into the saucepan, place over medium heat, and cook, whisking constantly, until thick. Pour the pastry cream into a large bowl, cover with plastic wrap, pressing the plastic onto the surface of the cream to prevent a skin from forming, and let cool until ready to use.

For the prenz, in a medium saucepan, whisk together 125 g (½ cup plus 2 tablespoons) of the granulated sugar and the cocoa powder.

In a second medium saucepan, whisk together the milk and the remaining granulated sugar then bring to a boil over medium heat. Remove from the heat and gradually pour the hot milk mixture over the cocoa mixture, whisking constantly until combined. Place the pan over medium heat and bring to a boil, stirring constantly to prevent sticking, until thick and glossy. Pour the prenz into a medium bowl, cover with plastic wrap, pressing the plastic onto the surface of the prenz to prevent a skin from forming, and refrigerate to set. (If needed, you can warm the prenz in the microwave or on the stove when ready to use it.)

To assemble and decorate the profiteroles, you will need two piping bags.

Using a stand mixer or handheld mixer, whip the double whipping cream until stiff peaks form. Divide the whipped cream in half and refrigerate one half for later use.

Add the remaining whipped cream to the reserved pastry cream and fold to combine. This is the chantilly cream that will be used to fill the Bignè. Transfer the chantilly cream to a piping bag with a round piping tip and fill the Bignè with the cream.

To create a pyramid with the Bignè, start by arranging a first round of Bignè as the base on a serving plate. Drizzle or spread a layer of prenz on top of the Bignè; the prenz will act as the glue between the layers of Bignè. Continue adding layers of Bignè and prenz, gradually moving inward to create the pyramid shape. There's no need to be precise at this point. Once the pyramid is complete, use a spoon to drizzle the prenz all over the pyramid to completely cover it. Refrigerate the pyramid for 10 to 15 minutes to set.

Transfer the remaining whipped cream to a pastry bag with a medium or small star tip.

Once the pyramid has set, finish decorating by piping the whipped cream into a motif you like all the way around the base of the pyramid. Profiteroles are best enjoyed the day they are made assembled, but any leftovers can be refrigerated for up to 2 days.

Biscotti ai pinoli

PINE NUT COOKIES

INGREDIENTS

Makes 15 to 20 cookies

For the almond paste

- 230 g (1½ cups plus 2 tablespoons) blanched whole almonds
- 200 g (1⅔ cups) icing sugar (confectioners' sugar), plus more as needed
- 40 g (1½ ounces) organic egg whites (about 1 large egg white)
- Zest of 1 organic lemon (optional)
- ½ teaspoon fine salt

For the cookies

- 300 g (1½ cups) granulated sugar
- Pinch of fine salt
- 90 g (3¼ ounces) organic egg whites (about 3 large eggs)
- 200 g (1⅔ cups) pine nuts
- Icing sugar (confectioners' sugar), for dusting

NOTE You can make the almond paste by hand, but I recommend using a food processor.

Ahhhhh, cookies!!!! How many recipes do you know? I have lost count. Cookies never fail to impress and this recipe makes one of the best cookies to enjoy during an afternoon tea. Pine nuts are such a treat! I remember, as a child, that my father appeared out of the blue one day to take me to the park. I didn't want to go with him, but he promised he would teach me something special. Now that I think about it, I know that he just wanted to chill on the grass. Because I was a chatterbox, he asked if I knew how birds whistle? When I said, "no", he explained that birds eat a lot of pine nuts, and if I ate lots of pine nuts, I would be able to whistle too. So, while he was dozing off under a tree, I searched for pinecones full of pine nuts and used a big rock to crush them and get the pine nuts. I saved some pine nuts in a bag, but I ate the rest. A few hours later, I tried to whistle and guess what? It worked! To this day, I don't want to know what really happened. It's nice to believe nice things. Kids should believe in fairy-tales and dreams, and adults, well, we should never stop dreaming either.

METHOD For the almond paste, in a food processor, combine the almonds with half of the icing sugar and blitz until the nuts are reduced to a fine flour. Add the remaining icing sugar and process until combined. Add the egg whites, lemon zest, if using, and the salt and process until the mixture forms a ball. If the mixture gets too sticky, add a little more icing sugar. Remove the paste from the food processor and shape it into a log then wrap in plastic wrap and refrigerate for 1 hour to set.

For the cookies, preheat the oven to 180°C (350°F). Line a baking sheet with parchment paper.

When the almond paste has chilled, break it into small chunks and place them in the bowl of a food processor. Add the granulated sugar and salt and blitz until combined. Add about half of the egg whites and process for about 100 seconds then gradually add the remaining egg whites in stages. The dough should be sticky but easy to roll into balls. Roll the dough into small balls weighing 20 to 25 g (¾ to 1 ounce) each. Use wet hands if the dough is too sticky.

Arrange the dough balls on the prepared baking sheet, leaving space for spreading. Place a few pine nuts on each ball. Dust the balls with icing sugar and bake for about 15 minutes, or until lightly golden. It's very important not to overbake these cookies—they should be light in colour and not too golden. Place the baking sheet on a rack and let the cookies cool at room temperature. The cookies can be stored in an airtight container at room temperature for up to 5 days.

Brioches col tuppo

SICILIAN BRIOCHES

METHOD In a small bowl, stir together the lemon zest, orange zest, rum, honey, and vanilla. Cover with plastic wrap and let stand at room temperature for 2 hours.

When the zest and vanilla mixture has stood for 2 hours, start making the brioche: Crumble the yeast into the bowl of a stand mixer fitted with the bread hook attachment. Add 100 ml (6 tablespoons plus 2 teaspoons) of the milk and mix on low until foamy. Add the sifted bread flour and mix on low until the flour starts to incorporate then add the granulated sugar, followed by the zest and vanilla mixture, and mix on low.

In a small bowl, gently whisk the 2 whole eggs just until combined.

With the mixer on low, gradually add the whisked whole eggs in three batches. With the mixer still on low, gradually add the butter in small batches, making sure the butter is fully incorporated before adding more.

Add the salt to the remaining milk. With the mixer still on low, carefully add the milk mixture to the dough then turn the mixer to medium and knead until a proper dough forms. Turn the mixer to high and knead until the dough stops sticking to the sides of the bowl.

Stop the mixer and let the dough fall out of the bowl onto a lightly floured work surface. Gently gather it into a ball, without touching it too much, and let it rest, uncovered, for 30 minutes.

When the dough has rested, use your hands to spread it on the lightly floured work surface. Gently spread the dough using your hands and start folding it into thirds (fold the left side towards the centre then fold the right side towards the centre). Rotate the dough one half turn towards you and gently shape

INGREDIENTS

Makes 10 brioches

- Zest of 1 organic lemon
- Zest of 1 organic orange
- 1 tablespoon light rum
- 1 tablespoon clear liquid honey, such as Acacia honey
- 1 teaspoon pure vanilla extract or paste (or the seeds of 1 vanilla bean pod)
- 12 g (^{2}/$_5$ ounce) fresh yeast (fresh brewer's yeast)
- 150 ml (½ cup plus 2 tablespoons) whole milk, plus 1½ tablespoons for the egg wash
- 430 g (3 cups plus 1 tablespoon) bread flour (or Manitoba flour), sifted
- 90 g (6 tablespoons) granulated sugar
- 2 large organic eggs, plus 1 large organic egg yolk for the egg wash
- 85 g (6 tablespoons) unsalted butter, at room temperature
- Pinch of fine salt

I have never been to Sicily, and believe me, I am very sorry about it. I intend to fix this very soon, not only because Sicily is known to be a very special place, where people are kind and warm and the environment is stunning, but also because food in Sicily is something from another world!
I can't wait to taste real Sicilian brioche, sliced in half and filled with almond gelato! Yes, brioche filled with gelato! It sounds like heaven on earth! This brioche recipe is not mine. It was given to me by a longtime friend from Palermo that has cooked real Sicilian food for me since I was a child. I know she will be happy to see her recipe in this book. Thank you, A.!

→

→

it into a ball, without stressing it too much or the air captured inside will be released and the brioche will be flat and dry. Place the dough in a large bowl, cover it with plastic wrap or a tea towel, and let it rise at room temperature for 1 hour then refrigerate it overnight.

The next morning, let the dough come to room temperature. Line a baking sheet with parchment paper.

Once the dough comes to room temperature, it will have doubled in volume. Place it on a lightly floured work surface and use a bread scraper or a large knife to divide it into ten equal pieces, weighing about 90 g (3¼ ounces) each. From each 90 g (3¼ ounce) piece, cut off a small 15 g (½ ounce) piece. Roll all the pieces into balls so there are ten larger balls and ten smaller balls.

Arrange the larger brioche balls on the prepared baking sheet, leaving space for expansion. Use your fingers to dig a small cavity in the centre of each ball then top each ball with one of the smaller balls, gently pressing it into the cavity. Loosely cover the baking sheet with plastic wrap and let the brioches rise at room temperature for about 1 hour, or until doubled in volume. (Once the brioches rise, they can be wrapped in plastic wrap and frozen for up to 3 months; When you want to bake them, remove them form the freezer and allow to defrost just a little (5 to 10 minutes), while you warm up the oven, then bake them while still frozen.

Preheat the oven to 180°C (350°F).

When the brioches have doubled in volume, in a small bowl, whisk together the remaining egg yolk and the remaining $1\frac{1}{2}$ tablespoons of milk. Gently brush the egg wash over each brioche then bake for about 17 minutes, or until beautifully golden. Place the baking sheet on a rack and let the brioches cool at room temperature. You can enjoy these brioches plain or slice them in half and spread your favourite gelato inside.

Tarte Tropézienne

INGREDIENTS

Makes 1 (20 cm / 8 inch) tart

For the orange sugar syrup
- 50 g (1¾ ounces) freshly squeezed orange juice
- 50 ml (3½ tablespoons) of water
- 2 tablespoons granulated sugar
- 1 teaspoon natural orange blossom water

For the brioche
- 12 (²/₅ ounce) fresh yeast (fresh brewer's yeast)
- 100 ml (6 tablespoons plus 2 teaspoons) whole milk, plus 1 tablespoon for the egg wash
- 300 g (2 cups plus 2 tablespoons) bread flour (or Manitoba flour)
- 3 tablespoons granulated sugar
- 1 teaspoon natural orange blossom water
- 1 teaspoon pure vanilla extract or paste (or the seeds of 1 vanilla bean pod)
- 3 large organic eggs, plus 1 large organic egg yolk for the egg wash
- 160 g (½ cup plus 3 tablespoons) unsalted butter, at room temperature
- ½ teaspoon fine salt
- Pearl sugar, for decoration

For the chantilly cream
- 2 large organic egg yolks
- 65 g (⅓ cup) granulated sugar
- 2½ tablespoons cornstarch, preferably organic
- 250 ml (1 cup plus 2 tablespoons) whole milk
- Peel of 1 organic lemon
- 1 teaspoon pure vanilla extract or paste (or the seeds of 1 vanilla bean pod)
- 250 g (1 cup plus 2 teaspoons) double whipping cream (heavy cream)

By the time I was 13, my mother had already had many surgeries. I lost count of how many. She had an accident before I was born and never really recovered, so hospitals were a constant presence in our life—my mother usually had to stay in the hospital for several months when she had surgery. At the time, France had the best orthopaedic doctors, so it was a popular place to have surgery. Usually, my mum went to France alone or with a friend, but when I was thirteen, she asked me if I wanted to join her, along with a friend she'd shared a hospital room with in the past and her friend's husband. We drove from Rome to Provence, heading towards Marseille, and once we made it to Saint-Tropez, we stopped at La Tarte Tropézienne, the very place where this recipe was invented. That day I had my first Tarte Tropézienne, and I was so struck, apparently, that I said: "When I grow up, I will bake cakes". Of course, I don't remember any of that, but what I do remember is the journey, the warm sun of the Riviera, the smell of beautiful flowers, the amazing food, and the fact that although it wasn't a "happy trip", we somehow managed to turn it into a day I won't easily forget.

METHOD For the orange sugar syrup, in a medium saucepan, bring the orange juice, water, granulated sugar, and orange blossom water to a boil over medium heat. Continue boiling until the sugar is completely dissolved. Let cool then refrigerate overnight.

For the brioche, crumble the yeast into the bowl of a stand mixer fitted with the bread hook attachment. Add 50 ml (3½ tablespoons) of the milk and mix on low until foamy. Sift the bread flour into the bowl and mix on low until the flour starts to incorporate then add the granulated sugar, followed by the orange blossom water and vanilla. Mix on low until incorporated.

In a small bowl, gently whisk the 3 whole eggs just until combined. With the mixer on low, gradually add the whisked whole eggs in three additions. With the mixer still on low, gradually add the butter in small additions, making sure it's fully incorporated before adding more.

Add the salt to the remaining milk then carefully add the mixture to the dough, turn the mixer to medium, and knead until a proper dough forms. Turn the

→

mixer to high and knead until the dough stops sticking to the sides of the bowl.

Stop the mixer and let the dough fall out of the bowl and onto a lightly floured work surface. Gently gather it into a ball, without touching it too much and let it rest, uncovered, for 30 minutes, or until doubled in volume.

When the dough has rested, use your hands to spread it on the lightly floured work surface. Gently spread the dough using your hands and start folding it into thirds (fold the left side towards the centre, then fold the right side towards the centre). Rotate the dough one half turn towards you and gently shape it into a ball, without stressing it too much or the air captured inside will be released and the brioche will be flat and dry. Place the dough in a large bowl, cover it with plastic wrap or a tea towel, and let it rise at room temperature for 1 hour then refrigerate it overnight.

For the chantilly cream, in a medium bowl, whisk together the egg yolks, granulated sugar, and cornstarch until pale.

In a medium saucepan, bring the milk and lemon peel to gentle boil over low heat. Remove the lemon peel then temper the egg mixture by slowly pouring a little milk into the bowl and stirring quickly. Pour the egg mixture into the saucepan, place over medium heat, and cook, stirring constantly, until thick. Remove from the heat and add the vanilla. Pour the pastry cream into a medium bowl, cover with plastic wrap, pressing the plastic onto the surface of the cream to prevent a skin from forming, and let cool at room temperature. Once cool, put the pastry cream in the fridge to set overnight.

The next morning, let the dough come to room temperature. Line a baking sheet with parchment paper.

When the dough has come to room temperature, it will have doubled in volume. Break the dough, pressing gently with your fist in the centre then invert it onto a lightly floured work surface. Use a rolling pin to roll out the dough into a perfect round that is about 4 cm (1½ inches) thick. Carefully transfer the dough to the prepared baking sheet. Cover it with a large bowl and let the brioche rise for about 1 hour, or until doubled in volume.

Preheat the oven to 180°C (350°F).

When the brioche has double in volume, in a small bowl, whisk together the remaining egg yolk and the remaining 1 tablespoon of milk. Gently brush the egg wash over the entire surface of the brioche then sprinkle the top with the pearl sugar. Bake for 25 minutes, or until lightly golden. Place the baking sheet on a rack and let the brioche cool at room temperature.

When the brioche is cool, use a long knife to cut it horizontally in half to create two layers. Pour the orange sugar syrup all over both cut surfaces and let it set while you prepare the filling.

To assemble the tart, fit a piping bag with a medium star pastry tip.

Using a stand mixer or handheld mixer, whip the double whipping cream until stiff peaks form. Fold the whipped cream into the pastry cream. This is the chantilly cream that will be used to fill the tart. Transfer the chantilly cream to the piping bag fitted with the star tip.

Arrange the bottom of the tart (the half without the pearl sugar) on a serving plate. Pipe curls or rosettes of chantilly cream all over the surface. (Alternatively, skip the piping bag and simply spread the cream all over the bottom.) Arrange the top of the tart over the chantilly cream. You did it! Enjoy!

Budini di riso

RICE PUDDING TARTELETTES

INGREDIENTS

Makes 8 tartelettes

For the pasta frolla

- 300 g (2½ cups plus 1 tablespoon) 00 flour
- 150 g (⅔ cup) unsalted butter, cold and cut into small pieces
- 120 g (½ cup plus 4 teaspoons) granulated sugar
- 1 large organic egg plus 2 large organic egg yolks
- Zest of 1 organic lemon
- 1 teaspoon pure vanilla extract or paste (or the seeds of 1 vanilla bean pod)

For the rice filling

- 350 ml (1¼ cups plus 3½ tablespoons) whole milk
- 60 g (¼ cup plus 2 teaspoons) granulated sugar
- Zest of 1 organic lemon
- Zest of 1 organic orange
- 1 teaspoon ground cinnamon (optional)
- Pinch of fine salt
- 80 g (6 tablespoons) round (short-grain) rice (or Japanese sushi rice)
- 25 g (5 teaspoons) unsalted butter

For the pastry cream

- 1 large organic egg
- 3 tablespoons granulated sugar
- 2 tablespoons cornstarch, preferably organic
- 200 ml (¾ cup plus 4 teaspoons) whole milk
- 1 teaspoon pure vanilla extract or paste (or the seeds of 1 vanilla bean pod)

- Icing sugar (confectioners' sugar), for decorating

Don't be mistaken. These tartelettes have nothing to do with the Rice Pudding (page 44) recipe I shared earlier in the chapter. They are called "budini", which translates to "puddings", but as a matter of fact, they are pastries. Originating from Tuscany, it's not clear whether budini di riso were created in Florence or Siena. They have a base made of pasta frolla, a sweet shortcrust pastry, and are filled with a cream that's made with rice, vanilla, and citrus. While they look like an afternoon treat, they are frequently eaten for breakfast. I often hear things like Italians never have cappuccino after 11:00 am, or certain pastries are only eaten in the afternoon and not in the morning. Nonsense! How about doing what you want, when you want, if it makes you happy?

METHOD For the pasta frolla, in the bowl of a food processor, combine the 00 flour and butter and blitz until sandy. Be careful not to over process the mixture or the blade will melt the butter. Add the granulated sugar, whole egg, egg yolks, lemon zest, and vanilla and blitz until a rough dough forms. Transfer the dough to a lightly floured work surface and knead it until smooth. Wrap the dough in plastic wrap and refrigerate it for at least 1 hour but preferably overnight.

For the rice filling, in a medium saucepan, bring the milk, granulated sugar, lemon zest, orange zest, cinnamon, if using, and the salt to a simmer over medium heat. Add the rice and cook for about 25 minutes, or until all the milk is absorbed, but the mixture still looks creamy. Add the butter and stir to melt. Remove from the heat and let cool completely at room temperature.

For the pastry cream, in a medium bowl, combine the egg, granulated sugar, and cornstarch and whisk until pale.

In a medium saucepan, bring the milk and vanilla to a gentle boil over medium heat. Temper the egg mixture by slowly pouring a little milk into the bowl and whisking quickly. Pour the egg mixture into the saucepan, place over medium

→

heat, and cook, whisking constantly, until thick. Pour the pastry cream into a large bowl, cover with plastic wrap, pressing the plastic onto the surface of the cream to prevent a skin from forming, and refrigerate until chilled.

Preheat the oven to 180°C (350°F). Grease the insides of 8 metal rice pudding moulds (or a muffin pan or more traditional oval metal moulds).

On a lightly floured work surface, use a rolling pin to roll out the pasta frolla until about 6 mm (¼ inch) thick. Using a 9 cm (3½ inch) round pastry cutter, cut the dough into circles. Line the inside of each mould with a pastry circle and place them on a baking sheet.

Add the cooled rice mixture to the chilled pastry cream mixture and stir until fully combined. Fill each pastry mould all the way to the top with the rice filling. Bake for 18 to 20 minutes then turn the oven temperature down to 165°C (325°F) and bake for 10 minutes more, or until lightly golden. Place the baking sheet on a rack and let the tartelettes cool completely. Sprinkle with icing sugar before serving. Budini di riso are best eaten the day they are made.

La mia Marble Cake

MY MARBLE CAKE

INGREDIENTS

**Makes 1 loaf
(23 x 13 cm / 9 x 5 inch)**

- 210 g (1½ cups) plain flour (all-purpose flour)
- 2½ teaspoons baking powder
- Pinch of fine salt
- 168 g (¾ cup) unsalted butter, at room temperature
- 300 g (1½ cups) granulated sugar
- 240 g (1 cup) cow's milk ricotta, at room temperature
- 2 teaspoons pure vanilla extract or paste (or the seeds of 2 vanilla bean pods)
- 3 large organic eggs, lightly beaten
- 30 g (6 tablespoons) unsweetened cocoa powder

For a long time, this cake has been my breakfast, my afternoon snack, and my after-dinner treat! It took me years and many failed attempts to bake it the way I like it. Although it's originally from Germany, almost every bakery in Rome makes a marble cake—it's earned a permanent place in our pastry tradition and I couldn't be happier about that. When I was a child, marble cake would fly from the kitchen counter in seconds. Back in the day, a big slice of this cake and a nice glass of cold milk with some cocoa sprinkled on top was what being a kid in Rome was all about. Germany, you know I love you, so please don't be mad that I've changed this recipe a little. You remain the country that created this simple yet not so easy to master recipe. I only added one of my favourite ingredients in baking, my beloved ricotta. Try it! The ricotta provides a very tender and light texture and once you taste my version, I reckon you will forgive me.

METHOD Preheat the oven to 170°C (335°F). Grease a 23 x 13 cm (9 x 5 inch) loaf pan then line it with parchment paper.

Sift the plain flour, baking powder, and salt into a medium bowl.

In the bowl of a stand mixer fitted with the paddle attachment, combine the butter and granulated sugar and beat on medium-high until pale and fluffy. Add the ricotta in two batches, followed by the vanilla. Add the eggs in three batches. Turn the mixer to low then add the flour mixture in three batches, being careful to not overbeat the batter. Divide the batter in half then add the cocoa powder to one portion and stir gently by hand until just combined. Place a spoonful of the vanilla cake batter in a corner of the prepared pan then place a spoonful of the chocolate cake batter next to it. Repeat to cover the entire base of the pan then repeat to create a second layer of batter, continuing until you run out of batter. Swirl a wooden stick inside the pan to roughly mix the two batters. Bake for 45 to 50 minutes, or until another wooden stick inserted in the centre of the cake comes out clean. Place the pan on a rack and let the cake cool completely. The marble cake can be wrapped in plastic wrap and stored in an airtight container at room temperature for up to 4 days.

Torta margherita

INGREDIENTS

Makes 1 cake
(21.5 cm / 8½ inch)

- 200 g (1½ cups plus 3 tablespoons) 00 flour
- 100 g (½ cup plus 2 tablespoons) potato starch
- 4 teaspoons baking powder
- 4 large organic eggs, separated
- 165 g (¾ cup plus 1½ tablespoons)
- 100 g (7 tablespoons) unsalted butter, melted and cooled
- 2 teaspoons pure vanilla extract or paste (or the seeds of 2 vanilla bean pods)
- 100 ml (6 tablespoons plus 2 teaspoons) whole milk, at room temperature
- 40 ml (2½ tablespoons plus 1 teaspoon) double whipping cream (heavy cream), at room temperature
- Pinch of fine salt
- Icing sugar (confectioners' sugar), for dusting

Originating from the northern Italian city of Pavia, this cake has very humble origins. It was made during the Christmas festivities in lieu of panettone and was often offered as a gift, but you can enjoy it for breakfast, with tea, or as a base for birthday or even wedding cakes. The name *margherita* means "daisy" and the colour and look of the cake are reminiscent of the pretty flower. Making this cake in winter was a way to look forward to the greatly anticipated spring season. While the original recipe didn't include dairy or other fats, over the years, the recipe was changed to improve the cake's texture, structure, and shelf life. The potato starch gives torta margherita its characteristic soft and light texture, so don't skip this important ingredient.

METHOD Preheat the oven to 170°C (335°F). Grease a 21.5 cm (8½ inch) springform pan then dust it with 00 flour. Sift the 00 flour and potato starch into a large bowl. Add the baking powder and whisk to combine.

In the bowl of a stand mixer fitted with the whisk attachment, beat the egg yolks and granulated sugar until doubled in volume. Add the melted and cooled butter and continue to beat then add the vanilla and beat until fully incorporated. Add the flour mixture in three additions then add the milk and double whipping cream and beat until fully incorporated.

In the bowl of a stand mixer fitted with the whisk attachment, or in a large bowl with an electric mixer, whip the egg whites and salt until stiff peaks form. Carefully fold the whipped egg whites into the batter, being careful to not deflate the egg whites. Carefully pour the batter into the prepared pan and bake for 45 to 50 minutes, or until a wooden pick inserted in the centre comes out clean. Place the pan on a rack and let the cake cool completely. Release and remove the sides of the pan and dust icing sugar all over the top of the cake then cut into slices and enjoy. Torta margherita is best enjoyed the day it is made but it can be stored in an airtight container at room temperature for up to 2 days.

Biscotti per il tè

AFTERNOON TEA COOKIES

INGREDIENTS

Makes about 20 cookies

For the pasta frolla

- 360 g (3 cups plus 1 tablespoon) 00 flour
- 180 g (1½ cups) icing sugar (confectioners' sugar)
- 140 g (⅔ cup plus 2 tablespoons) potato starch
- 256 g (1 cup plus 2 tablespoons) unsalted butter, cold and cut into small pieces
- 1 large organic egg plus 1 large organic egg yolk
- 1½ teaspoons pure vanilla extract or paste (or the seeds of 1½ vanilla bean pod)

For the chocolate glaze

- 350 g (12¼ ounces) dark chocolate, preferably 60% cacao, melted
- 1 teaspoon unsalted butter

NOTE I prefer to use a food processor to make the pasta frolla, because it speeds up the process, but you can make it by hand. Place the 00 flour, icing sugar, potato starch, and butter on a work surface and use your hands to rub the butter into the dry mixture until sandy then add the remaining ingredients and use your hands to incorporate them and create a rough dough.

I have yet to find a person who doesn't like this type of cookie. Every country has its own variation, and every kid loves them, while adults feel like children again when they eat them. Some people eat the chocolate part first, leaving the vanilla for last; some people dunk the chocolate part in a cup of hot tea or coffee, until the chocolate starts to melt; and some people just eat them whole! Personally, I eat the vanilla cookie part first and then the chocolate. I like to leave the best for last and extend the pleasure. Between me and you: I can eat tons of these!

METHOD For the pasta frolla, in the bowl of a food processor, combine the 00 flour, icing sugar, potato starch, and butter and blitz until sandy. Be careful not to over process the mixture or the blade will melt the butter. Add the whole egg, egg yolk, and vanilla and blitz until a rough dough forms. Transfer the dough to a lightly floured work surface and knead it until smooth. Wrap the dough in plastic wrap and refrigerate it for at least 1 hour but preferably overnight.

When the dough has chilled, preheat the oven to 180°C (350°F). Line one or two baking sheets with parchment paper.

On a lightly floured work surface, use a rolling pin to roll out the dough until about 6 mm (¼ inch) thick. Use your favourite cookie cutters to cut the dough into shapes then place the cookies on the prepared baking sheet. If the room is warm, place the cookies back in the fridge to firm up briefly before baking. Otherwise, bake for 8 to 15 minutes, or until pale and not all golden. Place the baking sheet on a rack and let the cookies cool completely.

For the chocolate glaze, using a bain-marie or in the microwave, melt the chocolate. Add the butter and stir until fully incorporated.

When the cookies are cool, dip one half of each cookie into the chocolate glaze. Lay the dipped cookies on a sheet of parchment paper to dry out. The cookies can be stored in an airtight container in the refrigerator for up to 3 days.

SOME MORE LESSONS

I AM LEARNING DAY BY DAY:

1. Consider the past a lesson to help you know how you want to live your present.

2. The present is never scary. You simply have to face it..

3. Growing up involves letting go of part of what you once were. And letting go is one of the most important weapons to carry through life.

4. Accept who you are and work on who you wish to become.

5. We are all damaged, but in our present, we can work on ourselves, adjusting the way we approach our thoughts and relate to others.

6. Whatever you do, put some love in it.

7. Every day is a potential new beginning.

8. Have the courage to rebel.

9. Have the guts to say no.

10. Don't do what the others do and don't follow trends. Instead, simply do whatever you wish to do the way you wish to do it. Get inspired by others but develop yourself.

11. Try to go to bed every night, being ok with whatever happened that day. If something needs to be changed, you will have time to do it tomorrow, but tomorrow is yet to come, so for now, sleep.

Melissa's
PRESENT

I have a very particular relationship with my fringe. I used to cut it really short whenever I felt empowered, ambitious, or feisty. It was a statement more than anything, a way to tell myself: "I am brave, I am strong"!

On the other hand, I used to let my fringe grow every time I felt sad, unmotivated, or lost. As I write this book, my fringe is longer, and I am thinking of getting rid of it completely—after 25 years! The funny thing is, this time I am contemplating letting it grow out, not because I am feeling sad or lost, but because I've learned that I don't need to be tough or ambitious to find my purpose or to prove myself. I've also learned that nothing is more important than the present and that facing the present with a softer approach, a more understanding and forgiving attitude towards myself and the world around me, makes me want to translate my interior change into a new hairstyle. It won't be easy, though. It's hard to let go of who we have been. It's confusing, unsettling, and scary, but really, if you think about it, the present is all we have.

I have grown and this is perhaps what scared me the most. It's easy to create a comfort zone and stay in it. Having the courage to move ahead is hard, and I realise now that I was terrified! After a great deal of panic and tears, I learned to spread my wings and allow myself to become who I am destined to be—a woman travelling through a new life.

My present defines my career abroad even more than my past. Although I started my journey in my native Italy, and still work there today, my career has always had an international element. This wasn't something I planned; it just happened that way, and I am extremely grateful for it. To be able to present my cakes in Italy, and around the world, gives me the privilege to share some of my country's traditions, as well as all the things I have learned through my travels.

Café Duse is now my proudest achievement. It is a place where I can finally see the new version of me. As in every recipe, all the ingredients are there: my cakes, my life, my style, my vision, and my attention to quality and details. Café Duse represents everything I have

prepared and worked for since the beginning of my career. It is a place where guests can get to know me and my story through my recipes and through every little detail I have personally selected. Duse is me but grown up.

The present looks less scary now, because I've learned that change is good, and change is necessary to thrive. The present is often tainted by our past or by our worries for the future, but really, is it worth it? Now, every day, I focus on the present. I stick to the now, because that is all we really have. When I dream about opening other shops, I realise I am leaving the present moment and so I stop and think about what I have now. The rest will come, as long as I keep moving.

I'm not worried about who I should become or constantly trying to prove myself. I refuse to spend my present worrying about my future. My present is about getting to know myself, but most of all, it is about my cakes. When I bake, every part of me is happy. I feel accomplished, I feel blessed, I am not scared of

"Nothing should be treasured more than the worth of each day."

JOHANN WOLFGANG VON GOETHE

anything, and the only thing I worry about in the near future is how long the cake needs to bake in the oven. I work one day at a time, trying to do what makes my heart warm and joyful, and the future will shape itself.

I am eager to see where the future takes me, but in the present moment, I am simply letting the journey unfold.

Scones per il tè senza uova

EGGLESS AFTERNOON TEA SCONES

INGREDIENTS

Makes 12 scones

- 380 g (3¼ cups) 00 flour
- 3 tablespoons granulated sugar
- 1 tablespoon baking powder
- 1 teaspoon baking soda
- Pinch of fine salt
- 100 g (7 tablespoons) unsalted butter, cold and cut into small pieces
- 250 ml (1 cup plus 2 teaspoons) buttermilk

NOTE If you can't find buttermilk, make your own: Combine 240 ml (1 cup) of whole milk and 3 teaspoons of white vinegar, stir, cover, and let stand until the milk curdles. Stir before using in place of normal buttermilk.

For scones with a more golden top, whisk an egg with a dash of milk and brush the mixture on each scone before baking.

You can make smaller scones, but you will need to adjust the baking time.

A piece of my heart remains in Scotland and will never leave. When I was young, I was obsessed with everything Scottish, from tartan fabrics and Scottish history to the country's castles and its landscape, but above all, Scottish pipes! Every time I hear their sound, I cry like a baby. The history of scones dates to 1500, when they were baked in large rounds then cut into quarters and cooked on the grill. Scottish scones differ from English scones, which often include fruit, eggs, and sugar. I have been baking this recipe for years. It's more Scottish than English, as it has no eggs and less sugar, resulting in a biscuit that's balanced, both savoury and sweet, quite rustic, and delicious. I always like my scones a bit irregular, well risen, and with a hint of savoury flavour. If you can find clotted cream serve your freshly baked scones with a good dollop of it and a teaspoon of strawberry jam, as tradition dictates. But if you can't find clotted cream, mascarpone works too.

METHOD Preheat the oven to 200°C (400°F). Line a baking sheet with parchment paper.

In the bowl of a food processor, combine the 00 flour, granulated sugar, baking powder, baking soda, and salt. Stir briefly with a spoon to mix. Add the butter and pulse until sandy. Be careful to not over process the dough; the secret to soft scones is mixing and touching the dough as little as possible. Transfer the mixture to a large bowl and add the buttermilk. Gently but quickly mix with either a fork or a spoon until a rough dough forms.

Drop the dough on a lightly floured work surface and gather it into a rough ball. It will look grainy, lumpy, and messy, but don't worry; it is meant to look like that. Using your hands, press the dough so it's roughly flat and about 3 cm (1¼ inch) thick. Using a 5 cm (2 inch) round, fluted pastry cutter, cut the dough into circles. (At this point, the scones can be wrapped in plastic wrap and frozen for up to 3 months. There is no defrosting needed before baking.)

Arrange the scones on the prepared baking sheet and bake for about 10 minutes, or until lightly golden. Place the baking sheet on a rack and let the scones cool briefly. Serve warm. The scones are best enjoyed the day they are baked.

Bignè mignon

INGREDIENTS
Makes 35 to 40 Bignè (puffs)

For the choux pastry
- 125 g (4⅓ ounce) whole milk
- 125 g (4⅓ ounce) water
- 100 g (7 tablespoons) unsalted butter, cut into small pieces
- ½ teaspoon granulated sugar
- Pinch of fine salt
- 150 g (1¼ cups) 00 flour
- 255 g (9 ounces) organic eggs (about 5 large eggs)
- Pearl sugar, for decorating

For the chantilly cream version
- 2 large organic egg yolks
- 65 g (⅓ cup) granulated sugar
- 2½ tablespoons cornstarch, preferably organic
- 250 ml (1 cup plus 2 teaspoons) whole milk
- Peel of 1 organic lemon
- 1 teaspoon pure vanilla extract or paste (or the seeds of 1 vanilla bean pod)
- 250 g (8¾ ounces) double whipping cream (heavy cream)

For the chocolate pastry cream version
- 5 large organic egg yolks
- 125 g (½ cup plus 2 tablespoons) granulated sugar
- 35 g (3½ tablespoons) cornstarch, preferably organic
- 20 g (¼ cup) unsweetened cocoa powder
- 500 g (17½ ounces) whole milk
- 125 g (4⅓ ounce) double whipping cream (heavy cream)
- 300 g (10½ ounces) dark chocolate, roughly chopped

NOTE At Café Duse, we offer these delicious treats in many different flavours. Here, I share two of our most beloved variations, one with chantilly cream and one with chocolate pastry cream. Choose the one you like the most or make them both—why not?

Pâte à choux is one of those miraculous preparations that surprise me every time! Each ingredient plays a very important role in the final result, but what really makes the difference is the technique and the method. The heat of the oven gives a push to the dough, lifting it up and making it as soft as a cloud! The eggs create a crunchy crust on the outside, while also balancing the texture and flavour. WOW! Just, WOW! With this recipe, you can make different versions, even savoury ones for a nice cocktail party bite—just reduce the sugar and add grated cheese. But these are the very popular treats you can find at Café Duse. They are so tiny that I can eat a dozen of them!

METHOD For the choux pastry, preheat the oven to 200°C (400°F). Line a baking sheet with parchment paper. Fit a piping bag with an Ateco 806 pastry tip or any medium round or star tip.

In a medium saucepan, bring the milk, water, butter, granulated sugar, and salt to a boil. Remove from the heat. Using a wooden spoon, quickly stir in the 00 flour. Place the pan over medium heat and cook, stirring constantly, for about 1 minute, or until you notice a film forming on the bottom of the pan and the back of the wooden spoon. Transfer the mixture to the bowl of a stand mixer fitted with the paddle attachment and let cool slightly.

In a small jug or bowl, briefly whisk the eggs.

With the mixer on low, gradually start adding the whisked eggs in stages. Continue mixing on low until the eggs are fully incorporated. The dough should have a thick and creamy texture, perfect for piping, and the bowl should feel warm but not too hot to the touch.

Transfer the dough to the prepared piping bag. Pipe small sized Bignè onto the prepared baking sheet, leaving a little space between each. Sprinkle the Bignè with a little pearl sugar and bake for 5 minutes. Lower the oven temperature to 180°C (350°F) and continue baking for 30 minutes more, or until lightly golden. Leave the Bignè in the oven with the door slightly open to dry out for about 10 minutes. Place the baking sheet on a rack and let the Bignè cool at room temperature.

For the chantilly cream version, fit a piping bag with a small star pastry tip.

In a medium bowl, combine the egg yolks, granulated sugar, and cornstarch and whisk until pale.

In a medium saucepan, bring the milk and lemon peel to a gentle boil over low heat. Remove the lemon peel. Temper the egg yolk mixture by slowly pouring a little milk into the bowl and stirring quick-

→

→

ly. Pour the egg mixture into the saucepan, place over medium heat, and cook, whisking constantly, until thick. Remove from the heat, add the vanilla, and stir to incorporate. Pour the pastry cream into a large bowl, cover with plastic wrap, pressing the plastic onto the surface of the cream to prevent a skin from forming, and let cool at room temperature then refrigerate until chilled.

Using a stand mixer or handheld mixer, whip the double whipping cream until stiff peaks form.

Fold the whipped cream into the chilled pastry cream then transfer it to the prepared piping bag.

Using a small, serrated knife, slice the Bignè crosswise in half. Pipe a dollop of the chantilly cream on each of the bottom halves then place the top halves on top of the cream. Pretty, uh?

For the chocolate pastry cream version, fit a piping bag with a medium round pastry tip.

In a medium bowl, combine the egg yolks, granulated sugar, cornstarch, and cocoa powder and whisk until fully combined.

In a medium pan, bring the milk and double whipping cream to a gentle boil over low heat. Temper the egg mixture by slowly pouring a little of the milk mixture into the bowl and whisking quickly. Pour the egg mixture into the saucepan, place over medium heat, and cook, whisking constantly, until thick. Remove from the heat, add 100 g (3½ ounces) of the chopped chocolate, and stir to melt. Pour the pastry cream into a large bowl, cover with plastic wrap, pressing the plastic onto the surface of the cream to prevent a skin from forming, and let cool at room temperature then refrigerate until chilled.

Transfer the chilled chocolate pastry cream to the prepared piping bag. Gently push the pastry tip into the bottom of each Bignè to create a hole and then squeeze the cream into the Bignè until they feel heavy.

In a bain-marie or in the microwave, melt the remaining chocolate. Let cool briefly then dip the top of each Bignè in the melted chocolate. Place the Bignè on a tray to dry. Enjoy!

Mignons alla frutta

MINI FRUIT TARTELETTES

INGREDIENTS

Makes about 30 mini tartelettes

For the pastry cream
- 2 large organic egg yolks
- 65 g (⅓ cup) granulated sugar
- 2½ tablespoons cornstarch, preferably organic
- Pinch of fine salt
- 500 ml (2 cups plus 1 tablespoon) whole milk
- 1 teaspoon pure vanilla extract or paste (or the seeds of 1 vanilla bean pod)

For the pastry dough
- 215 g (¾ cup plus 3 tablespoons) unsalted butter, at room temperature
- 308 g (2½ cups plus 1 tablespoon) icing sugar (confectioners' sugar)
- 180 g (6½ ounces) organic eggs (about 8 large eggs) plus 40 g (1½ ounces) organic egg yolks (about 2 large egg yolks)
- ¼ tsp fine salt
- 1 teaspoon pure vanilla extract or paste (or the seeds of 1 vanilla bean pod)
- Zest of 1 organic lemon
- 460 g (3⅓ cups) plain flour (all-purpose flour)
- 75 g (6 tablespoons) fine corn flour, preferably organic (not polenta)

For the fruit topping
- Mixed berries or other fresh fruit
- Apricot jam

A classic of Italian pastry culture, these fresh, versatile, sweet, and above all, super pretty little treats excite kids and delight adults. They can be found in every pastry shop in Italy, but also at Café Duse, of course. These tartelettes are very delicate and mild in flavour, so each ingredient must be top quality. Trust me, you will taste the difference! Make them for cocktail parties, birthdays, or any special event. Bring them as a gift to a friend's dinner, serve them with your favourite afternoon beverage, or start the day on a Sunday morning in the most delicious way!

METHOD For the pastry cream, in a medium bowl, combine the egg yolks, granulated sugar, cornstarch, and salt and whisk until pale.

In a medium saucepan, bring the milk and vanilla to a gentle boil over medium heat. Temper the egg yolk mixture by slowly pouring a little milk into the bowl and stirring quickly. Pour the egg yolk mixture into the saucepan, place over medium heat, and cook, whisking constantly, until thick. Remove from the heat. Pour the pastry cream into a medium bowl, cover with plastic wrap, pressing the plastic onto the surface of the cream to prevent a skin from forming, and let cool at room temperature until ready to use.

For the pastry dough, in the bowl of a stand mixer fitted with the paddle attachment, beat the butter and the icing sugar until creamy.

In a small bowl, combine the whole eggs and egg yolks and whisk briefly. Gradually add the egg mixture to the butter mixture, followed by the salt, vanilla, and lemon zest, and beat on low to incorporate. Add the plain flour and corn flour and beat low at first, then medium just until a dough forms, being careful to not overbeat the dough. Transfer the dough to a lightly floured work surface and gather it into a ball. Wrap the dough in plastic wrap and refrigerate it for at least 1 hour.

→

→

Preheat the oven to 170°C (335°F). Brush three mini muffin pans or 30 mini tartelette moulds with butter or spray with baking spray.

When the dough has chilled, on a lightly floured work surface, use a rolling pin to roll out the dough until about 6 mm (¼ inch) thick. Use a 4 cm (1½ inch) round pastry cutter to cut the dough into rounds. Fit each round into a mini muffin pan cavity or tartelette mould, removing any excess dough. Bake for 10 to 15 minutes, or until the mini tartelette shells are pale with lightly golden edges. Place the muffin pans or tartelette moulds on a rack and let the mini tartelette shells cool completely.

When the mini tartelette shells are cool, fill each tartelette with a little pastry cream then top with fresh fruit.

In a small saucepan, warm a little apricot jam over low heat then press it through a fine-mesh sieve set over a bowl. Discard any chunks of fruit. Brush the warm jam on the fruit to give it a nice glaze. Enjoy right away. These tartelettes are best eaten the day they are made but can be stored in an airtight container in the refrigerator for up to 1 day.

Torta tiramisù a modo mio

TIRAMISÙ MY WAY

INGREDIENTS

Makes 1 (20 cm / 8 inch) cake

Makes about 12 servings

For the cake

- 280 g (2 cups) plain flour (all-purpose flour)
- 1½ teaspoons baking powder
- 200 g (1 cup) caster sugar (superfine sugar)
- 4 large organic eggs, separated and at room temperature
- ¼ teaspoon cream of tartar
- 200 ml (¾ cup plus 4 teaspoons) strong brewed coffee, at room temperature
- 100 ml (6 tablespoons plus 2 teaspoons) vegetable oil, preferably non-GMO
- 1 teaspoon pure vanilla extract or paste (or the seeds of 1 vanilla bean pod)
- Pinch of fine salt

For the mascarpone frosting

- 250 ml (1 cup plus 2 teaspoons) double whipping cream (heavy cream)
- 250 g (8¾ ounces) mascarpone cheese
- 90 g (¾ cup) icing sugar (confectioners' sugar)
- Unsweetened cocoa powder, for dusting

I've been asked, once again, to share this recipe. In some ways, this cake made my fortune, so I am very grateful to this recipe and to all the people who have made it and shared it on social media. Thank you! For those of you baking it for the first time, allow me to give you a few tips. Although this recipe is simple, it can be tricky. Fat helps provide structure in cakes, but there is very little fat in this recipe, so it is very important that the ingredients are at room temperature. You also need to be very gentle when mixing the ingredients together so you keep as much air in the batter as possible, which will give this cake the proper height. Finally, don't overmix the batter. If you follow these tips, you will succeed!

METHOD For the cake, preheat oven to 180°C (350°F). Butter two 20 cm (8 inch) round cake pans then line the bottoms with parchment paper.

Sift the plain flour into a medium bowl. Add the baking powder and 100 g (½ cup) of the caster sugar and whisk to combine.

In a large bowl, combine the egg whites and cream of tartar.

In the bowl of a stand mixer fitted with the paddle attachment, combine the egg yolks, 100 ml (6 tablespoons plus 2 teaspoons) of the coffee, the vegetable oil, vanilla, and salt and beat until combined. Add the flour mixture and beat for 1 minute, or just until well incorporated; do not overmix the batter.

Using an electric mixer (or a stand mixer fitted with the whisk attachment), whip the egg whites and cream of tartar until frothy then add the remaining caster sugar and whip until stiff peaks form. Very gently fold the whipped egg whites into the batter; the batter will be very pale. Carefully divide the batter between the prepared pans and bake for 20 to 25 minutes, or until a wooden pick inserted in the centre of each cake comes out clean.

→

→

Remove the cakes from the oven and use a pastry brush to brush some of the remaining coffee on top of both. Wait about 2 minutes to let the coffee soak in then invert the cakes onto a rack and let them cool completely.

For the mascarpone frosting, in the bowl of a stand mixer fitted with the whisk attachment, whip the double whipping cream until medium stiff peaks form. Do not overbeat the cream or it will curdle. Transfer the cream to a large bowl and refrigerate it while you make the rest of the frosting.

Put the mascarpone and the icing sugar in the same bowl of the stand mixer, switch to the paddle attachment, and beat until creamy. Add the chilled whipped cream and beat to combine.

To assemble the cake, brush more of the coffee on both cakes. Place one cake layer on a cake board or serving plate and use a rubber spatula to spread some of the mascarpone frosting on top. Generously dust the cake with cocoa powder then place the second cake layer on top. Using a straight metal spatula, spread the remaining frosting over the top and sides of the cake. I like this cake to be simple, so I usually don't add any decoration, but I use a cake scraper to smooth the top and sides and then I give the top a generous dust of cocoa powder. This way the cake will resemble the original Tiramisù dessert. Place in the fridge until ready to serve. The Tiramisù can be stored in the refrigerator for up to 3 days.

Torta Red Velvet di Melissa

MY SECRET RECIPE

MELISSA'S RED VELVET CAKE

INGREDIENTS

Makes 1 (20 cm / 8 inch) cake
Makes about 12 servings

For the cake

· 200 ml (¾ cup plus
  4 teaspoons) whole milk,
  at room temperature
· 100 ml (6 tablespoons
  plus 2 teaspoons) apple
  cider vinegar
· 1 tablespoon all-natural
  vegetarian (cochineal-free)
  red food colouring gel or paste
· 385 g (2¾ cups) plain flour
  (all-purpose flour)
· 40 g (½ cup) unsweetened
  cocoa powder
· 2 teaspoons baking soda
· ¼ teaspoon fine salt
· 400 ml (1⅔ cups) vegetable
  oil, preferably non-GMO
· 450 g (2¼ cups)
  granulated sugar
· 2 teaspoons pure vanilla
  extract or paste (or the
  seeds of 2 vanilla bean pods)
· 4 large organic eggs

For the frosting

· 256 g (1 cup plus
  2 tablespoons) unsalted
  butter, at room temperature
· 500 g (17½ ounces)
  spreadable cream cheese, cold
· 1 teaspoon pure vanilla
  extract or paste (or the
  seeds of 1 vanilla bean pod)
· 250 g (2 cups plus
  1 tablespoon) icing sugar
  (confectioners' sugar)

NOTE In this recipe I use food
colouring. Of course, it must
be all natural and vegetarian.
If you can't find it in shops,
search the internet. There are
many brands producing natural colours available online. I
don't recommend powder colours, which create a brown tone
rather than red. Instead, use a
gel or paste. You can also use
beetroots, but the cake will be
darker in colour and most of all,
it will have a different flavour.

This has been my most popular recipe since I started my pastry career
15 years ago! Everywhere I go and every
time I make it, my guests go crazy for it.
I have been asked to share the recipe for
many years but kept it a secret since the
moment I created it. I've finally decided
that it's time to share the recipe, and I
couldn't be happier about it. I must be
honest and tell you that this is a very
rich cake, made with a lot of sugar and
fat—that is what makes it so good! You
can save this cake for very special occa-
sions, and I guarantee it will be a pure
success. And it's so easy to make! In my
Christmas book, I shared the vegan version, but this is the original red velvet
cake you can find at Café Duse!

METHOD For the cake, preheat the oven
to 170°C (335°F). Grease two 20 cm (8
inch) round cake pans then line the bottoms with parchment paper.

In a medium bowl, combine the milk,
apple cider vinegar, and red food colouring and stir vigorously to combine.
Cover and let stand at room temperature for at least 8 minutes. This is your
homemade buttermilk. It will look like
red sour milk, but it is meant to look
that way. Do not worry!

Sift the plain flour into a large bowl then
add the cocoa powder, baking soda, and
salt. Whisk to combine.

In another large bowl, combine the vegetable oil, granulated sugar, and vanilla
and whisk to fully combine. Add the
eggs, one at a time, and whisk to incorporate. Add the flour mixture in three
additions then add the red buttermilk
and whisk until the batter looks dense
and red. Carefully divide the batter between the prepared pans and bake for
40 to 45 minutes, or until a wooden
pick inserted in the centre of each cake
comes out clean. Place the pans on a
rack and let the cakes cool then invert
the cakes onto the rack and let them
cool completely.

→

→

For the frosting, in the bowl of a stand mixer fitted with the paddle attachment, beat the butter on low until creamy. With the mixer on low, gradually add the cream cheese, followed by the vanilla, and beat until combined. Sift the icing sugar into the bowl and beat until fully combined. Place the frosting in the fridge to chill and set for about 15 minutes.

To assemble the cake, place one cake layer on a cake board or serving plate. If your cake has developed a dome shape, use a serrated knife to trim the excess and make it flat. Use your fingers to break the trimmed extras into cake crumbles and reserve them for decorating. Use a rubber spatula to spread some of the frosting on top then place the second cake layer on top. Using an offset spatula, spread the remaining frosting over the top and sides of the cake. Sprinkle the reserved cake crumbles over the surface of the cake anyway you please. Refrigerate the cake for about 30 minutes to set the frosting then cut it into slices and serve. The Red Velvet Cake can be stored in the refrigerator for up to 3 days.

La mia torta alle carote

MY CARROT CAKE

INGREDIENTS

Makes 1 (20 cm / 8 inch) cake
Makes about 12 servings

For the cake

- 500 g (17½ ounces) carrots, trimmed and peeled
- 180 g (6½ ounces) canned pineapple, roughly chopped
- 90 g (¾ cup) pecans, roughly chopped, plus more for decorating
- Zest and juice of 1 organic orange
- 1 teaspoon ground cinnamon
- 2 cloves
- Pinch of ground nutmeg
- 4 large organic eggs
- 350 g (1¾ cups) granulated sugar
- 225 ml (¾ cup plus 3 tablespoons) vegetable oil, preferably non-GMO
- 1½ teaspoons pure vanilla extract or paste (or the seeds of 1½ vanilla bean pods)
- 300 g (2 cups plus 2 tablespoons) plain flour (all-purpose flour)
- 2 teaspoons baking soda
- 2 teaspoons baking powder
- Pinch of fine salt

For the frosting

- 256 g (1 cup plus 2 tablespoons) unsalted butter, at room temperature
- 500 g (17½ ounces) spreadable cream cheese, cold
- 1 teaspoon pure vanilla extract or paste (or the seeds of 1 vanilla bean pod)
- 250 g (2 cups plus 1 tablespoon) icing sugar (confectioners' sugar)

I love this cake!!! It's so rich and full of flavour, not to mention vitamin C! While it is indulgent, you can always be sensible and have a small slice from time to time. If you happen to like dry cakes, well, this is not for you. This cake is moist. Yes, very moist! I've heard that many people don't like the sound of this word, but I don't mind it. When it comes to cakes, being moist is rule number one for me.

METHOD For the cake, preheat the oven to 180°C (350°F). Grease two 20 cm (8 inch) round cake pans then line the bottoms with parchment paper.

Using a large grater or a food processor, grate the carrots. Transfer to a large bowl then add the pineapple, pecans, orange zest and juice, cinnamon, cloves, and nutmeg. Use your hands to fully combine.

In the bowl of a stand mixer fitted with the whisk attachment, combine the eggs and granulated sugar and whip on high until doubled in volume and very pale in colour. With the mixer on low, add the vegetable oil in a slow, steady stream and mix until fully incorporated. Add the vanilla and mix for 1 more minute. Turn the mixer off then add the plain flour, baking soda, baking powder, and salt and mix on low until just combined; do not overmix the batter. If you see streaks of flour here and there, leave them—it's ok. Add the carrot mixture and use a wooden spoon or rubber spatula to fold the ingredients together. Divide the batter between the prepared pans and bake for 40 to 45 minutes, or until a wooden pick inserted in the cen-

→

→

tre of each cake comes out clean. Place the pans on a rack and let the cakes cool then invert the cakes onto the rack and let them cool completely.

For the frosting, in the bowl of a stand mixer fitted with the paddle attachment, beat the butter on low until creamy. With the mixer on low, gradually add the cream cheese, followed by the vanilla, and beat until combined. Sift the icing sugar into the bowl and beat until fully combined. Place the frosting in the fridge to chill and set for about 15 minutes.

To assemble the cake, place one cake layer on a cake board or serving plate. Use a rubber spatula to spread some of the frosting on top then place the second cake layer on top. Using an off-set spatula, spread the remaining frosting over the top and sides of the cake. Decorate the cake with some whole pecans. Refrigerate the cake for about 30 minutes to set the frosting then cut it into slices and serve. The Carrot Cake can be stored in the refrigerator for up to 3 days.

Mignons al limone e pinoli

LEMON AND PINE NUT TARTELETTES

INGREDIENTS

**Makes 25 to 30
mini tartelettes**

For the lemon curd filling

- 2 large organic eggs
- 1 teaspoon cornstarch,
  preferably organic
- 2 medium organic lemons
- 140 g (⅔ cup plus 2
  teaspoons) granulated sugar
- 113 g (½ cup) unsalted butter

For the pastry dough

- 215 g (¾ cup plus
  3 tablespoons) unsalted
  butter, at room temperature
- 308 g (2½ cups plus
  1 tablespoon) icing sugar
  (confectioners' sugar)
- 180 g (6½ ounces)
  organic whole eggs
  (about 8 large eggs)
  plus 40 g (1½ ounces)
  organic egg yolks (about 2
  large egg yolks)
- Zest of 1 organic lemon
- 1 teaspoon pure vanilla
  extract or paste (or the
  seeds of 1 vanilla bean pod)
- ¼ teaspoon fine salt
- 460 g (3⅓ cups) plain
  flour (all-purpose flour)
- 75 g (6 tablespoons)
  fine corn flour, preferably
  organic (not polenta)
- 70 to 80 g (2½ to 2¾ ounces)
  pine nuts, for decorating

NOTE Be sure to toast the pine
nuts–it releases their natural oils.

These treats are inspired by the classic torta della nonna, or "Grandma's cake". In addition to transforming this cake into tartelettes, I also wanted to give it a lift and decided to fill these little tartelettes with fresh and tangy lemon curd instead of a milder pastry cream. I find these changes created a winner!

METHOD For the lemon curd, in a medium bowl, briefly whisk the eggs then add the cornstarch and whisk to incorporate.

Use a sharp knife to cut the peel from the lemons and place it in a medium saucepan. Squeeze the lemons into the saucepan, then add the granulated sugar and butter and bring to a gentle boil over medium heat. Temper the egg mixture by slowly pouring a little of the lemon mixture into the bowl and stirring quickly. Pour the egg mixture into the saucepan, place over low heat, and cook, stirring constantly, until thick. Remove from the heat, remove the lemon peel with a fork, and pour the curd through a fine-mesh sieve set over a bowl. Cover with plastic wrap, pressing the plastic onto the surface of the curd to prevent a skin from forming, and let it cool at room temperature for 1 hour then refrigerate overnight.

The next day, remove the curd from the fridge and stir it briefly then set it aside until ready to use.

For the pastry dough, in the bowl of a stand mixer fitted with the paddle attachment, beat the butter and icing sugar on medium at first then high until fluffy and creamy.

In a small bowl, combine the whole eggs and egg yolks and whisk briefly. Gradually add the egg mixture to the butter

→

mixture, followed by the lemon zest, vanilla, salt, and beat on low to incorporate. Add the plain flour and corn flour and beat on low at first and then medium until a dough is formed, being careful not to overbeat the dough. Transfer the dough to a lightly floured work surface and gather it into a ball. Wrap the dough in plastic wrap and refrigerate it for at least 1 hour.

Preheat the oven to 170°C (335°F). Brush three mini muffin pans or 30 mini tartelette moulds with butter or spray with baking spray. Line a baking sheet with parchment paper.

When the dough has chilled, on a lightly floured work surface, use a rolling pin to roll out the dough until about 6 mm (¹/₄ inch) thick. Use a 4 cm (1½ inch) round pastry cutter to cut the dough into rounds. Fit each round into a mini muffin pan cavity or tartelette mould, removing any excess dough. Bake for about 8 minutes, or until the mini tartelettes shells are pale with lightly golden edges. Place the muffin pans or tartelette moulds on a rack and let the mini tartelette shells cool completely. Leave the oven on.

While the tartelette shells are cool, spread the pine nuts on the prepared baking sheet and toast them in the oven temperature until lightly golden.

Fill each tartelette with a dollop of lemon curd and top with some toasted pine nuts. Serve on a beautiful tray and enjoy! These tartelettes are best enjoyed the day they are made.

Biscotti occhi di bue

SANDWICH COOKIES

INGREDIENTS
Makes 4 large cookies

For the pasta frolla
- 256 g (1 cup plus 2 tablespoons) unsalted butter, at room temperature
- 250 g (2 cups plus 1 tablespoon) icing sugar (confectioners' sugar)
- 2 large organic eggs
- 1 teaspoon pure vanilla extract or paste (or the seeds of 1 vanilla bean pod)
- 500 g (4¼ cups) 00 flour

For decorating
- Your favourite jam
- Icing sugar (confectioners' sugar)

NOTE The secret to making perfect occhi di bue is to remove the cookies from the oven when they are still very pale and let them cool completely before touching them.

Almost every country has a cookie like this one in its baking repertoire. In Austria, Linzer cookies are something to die for—they are also enjoyed in Germany—while in the United States and England they make thumbprint cookies, and in Italy the name occhi di bue, literally means "bull's eyes", due to their particular shape. Traditionally, these cookies can be found in pretty much every pastry shop in Italy. Filled with jam or hazelnut spread and often dusted with icing sugar or decorated with chocolate, they are excellent for an afternoon tea and beautiful as a Christmas present. Why have I chosen to include this popular recipe? Because it reminds me, once again, about when I was a child, and I used to eat one giant cookie, filled with jam, at the local pastry shop while waiting for my mother to pick me up after school. You can bake them small or medium, but I share with you my favourite version, which is, of course, huge, just like the one I used to eat during my childhood.

METHOD For the pasta frolla, in the bowl of a stand mixer fitted with the paddle attachment, combine the butter and icing sugar and beat on medium until combined and then on high until pale and fluffy. Add the eggs, one at a time, followed by the vanilla and then the 00 flour and beat until just combined, being careful to not overmix the dough or it will separate. Transfer the dough to a lightly floured work surface and gather it into a ball. Wrap the dough in plastic wrap and refrigerate it for at least 2 hours but preferably overnight.

When the dough has chilled, preheat the oven to 180°C (350°F). Line a baking sheet with parchment paper.

On a lightly floured work surface, use a rolling pin to roll out the dough until about 6 mm (¼ inch) thick. Use a 6 cm (2½ inch) round cookie cutter to cut the dough into rounds. Using the back of a medium piping tip or a small round cookie cutter, cut smaller rounds into half of the cookies to create cookie rings and small rounds. Arrange the cookies on the prepared baking sheet and bake for about 12 minutes, until firm but still pale. (You can bake the smaller rounds of dough into delicious miniature cookies, so nothing goes to waste.) Place the baking sheet on a rack and let the cookies cool completely.

When the cookies are cool, fill a piping bag fitted with a small or medium round pastry tip with your favourite jam. Pipe a small dollop of jam in the centre of the larger round cookies (the ones without small rounds cut out), leaving a border around the edge.

Place some icing sugar on a plate. Take the cookie rings (the rounds with the centres cut out) and dip them, one by one, in the icing sugar. Place the icing sugar–dusted cookie rings on top of the jam-covered rounds and sandwich them together. Enjoy right away! Occhi di bue can be stored in an airtight container in the fridge for 4 to 5 days.

Mignons al caffè

MINI COFFEE ÉCLAIRS

INGREDIENTS

Makes about 20 mini éclairs

For the coffee pastry cream

- 6 large organic egg yolks
- 215 g (1 cup plus
  1 tablespoon)
  granulated sugar
- 60 g (6 tablespoons)
  cornstarch, preferably
  organic
- 600 ml (2½ cups) whole milk
- 100 ml (6 tablespoons plus
  2 teaspoons) strong brewed
  coffee, at room temperature
- 1 teaspoon pure vanilla
  extract or paste (or the
  seeds of 1 vanilla bean pod)

For the mignons

- 4 large organic eggs
- 250 ml (1 cup plus
  2 teaspoons) water
- 75 g (⅓ cup) unsalted butter
- 1 teaspoon granulated sugar
- ¼ teaspoon fine salt
- 150 g (1¼ cups) 00 flour

For decorating

- 200 g (7 ounces) fondant
- 2 teaspoons coffee liqueur
  of your choice
- Coffee beans (optional)

NOTE The coffee cream recipe yields a little more than you need, but you can use the leftovers in other treats, and it can be frozen for up to a month.

Pâte à choux, coffee, and cream are three of my all-time favourites! And they all come together in these perfect miniature éclairs. I must confess that this recipe requires quite a few steps, but the extra effort is definitely worth it. If you prefer, you can come to Café Duse, and find them freshly baked every morning. I won't say anymore—let's begin!

METHOD For the coffee pastry cream, in a large bowl, combine the egg yolks, granulated sugar, and cornstarch and whisk until pale.

In a large saucepan, bring the milk, coffee, and vanilla to a gentle boil over low heat. Temper the egg yolk mixture by slowing pouring a little of the milk mixture into the bowl and whisking quickly. Pour the egg mixture into the saucepan, place over medium heat, and cook, whisking constantly until thick. Pour the pastry cream into a large bowl, cover with plastic wrap, pressing the plastic onto the surface of the cream to prevent a skin from forming, and refrigerate it until set, at least 2 hours but preferably overnight.

For the mignons, preheat the oven to 190°C (375°F). Line a baking sheet with parchment paper. Fit a piping bag with a medium round or star pastry tip.

In a small jug or bowl, briefly whisk the eggs.

In a large saucepan, bring the water, butter, granulated sugar, and salt to a boil. Remove from the heat. Using a wooden spoon, quickly stir in all the 00 flour and continue stirring vigorously until the flour has been completely absorbed and you can see a film on the back of the wooden spoon. Transfer the mixture to the bowl of a stand mixer fitted with the paddle attachment. With the mixer on

→

low, gradually add the whisked eggs in stages. (If you don't have a stand mixer, you can use a bowl and an electric mixer or beat the eggs in by hand.) Continue beating until the bowl feels warm but not too hot and most of the humidity has evaporated from the batter.

Transfer the dough to the prepared piping bag and pipe the dough into thick roughly 2.5 cm (1 inch) long, éclairs, leaving about 2 cm (¾ inch) of space between them. Bake for 15 minutes then lower the oven temperature to 170°C (335°F) and bake for about 10 more minutes, or until nicely golden. Place the baking sheet on a rack and let the éclairs cool at room temperature.

When ready to fill the éclairs, fit a piping bag with a small round pastry tip.

Remove the coffee pastry cream from the fridge and give it a good stir. Transfer the cream to the prepared piping bag. Gently push the pastry tip into the bottom of each éclair to create a hole then squeeze the cream into the éclairs until they feel heavy.

To decorate the éclairs, warm the fondant in a large bowl set over a pan of simmering water, making sure the bowl doesn't touch the water. Add the coffee liqueur and stir to incorporate. Dip the top of each éclair in the melted fondant and let dry. Top each éclair with a coffee bean, if desired. Enjoy! The éclairs are best enjoyed the day they are made but will keep in an airtight container in the refrigerator for up to 1 day.

Torta sapore di Sicilia

A CAKE INSPIRED BY SICILY

INGREDIENTS

Makes 1 (20 cm / 8 inch) cake
Makes about 12 servings

For the cake

- 325 g (2¼ cups plus ½ tablespoon) plain flour (all-purpose flour), sifted
- 1 tablespoon baking powder
- 1 teaspoon ground cinnamon, plus more for decorating
- Pinch of fine salt
- 180 g (¾ cup plus 1 tablespoon) unsalted butter, at room temperature
- 300 g (1½ cups) granulated sugar
- 180 g (¾ cup) sour cream, at room temperature
- 2 teaspoons pure vanilla extract or paste (or the seeds of 2 vanilla bean pods)
- 6 large organic egg whites
- 180 ml (¾ cup) buttermilk (see note on page 88 for how to make your own)
- 60 ml (¼ cup) water

For the ricotta filling

- 320 g (1⅓ cups) cow's milk ricotta, strained if watery
- 285 g (1 cup plus 3 tablespoons) mascarpone
- 150 g (1¼ cups) icing sugar (confectioners' sugar)
- 100 g (½ cup plus 1 tablespoon) mini chocolate chips, plus more for decorating

For the mascarpone frosting

- 560 g (2⅓ cups) mascarpone
- 280 g (2⅓ cups) icing sugar (confectioners' sugar)

I created this recipe as a tribute to one of the greatest regions in Italy, Sicily, but mostly, I wanted something to remind me of the Sicilian cannoli, without having to make them! I adore cannoli's cinnamon and chocolate flavour, and the creamy ricotta filling is pure heaven to me, but making cannoli is a very time-consuming process. Another reason I don't make cannoli is that the traditional recipe calls for strutto (lard). Being vegetarian, I don't use lard in my recipes, and I have so much respect for the original recipe, I didn't want to substitute lard with other ingredients. For those of you who don't mind lard, do yourself a favour and go to Sicily to try the real deal! You will be absolutely hooked! Alternatively, this tall and beautiful layer cake captures all the right flavours without the hassle—well, a little work is still required. I hope you enjoy it!

METHOD For the cake, preheat the oven to 170°C (335°F). Grease two 20 cm (8 inch) round cake pans then line the bottoms with parchment paper.

Sift the plain flour into a large bowl then add the baking powder, cinnamon, and salt and whisk to combine.

In the bowl of a stand mixer fitted with the paddle attachment, beat the butter and granulated sugar until very pale and fluffy. Add the sour cream and vanilla and beat until fully combined. With the mixer on low, add the egg whites, one at a time, and beat until incorporated.

Meanwhile, in a medium bowl, whisk the buttermilk and water. Add this mixture to the butter mixture and beat until fully combined Add the flour mixture and beat just until incorporated. Scrape down the sides of the bowl then divide the batter between the prepared pans. Bake for 20 to 25 minutes, or until a wooden pick inserted in the centre of each cake comes out clean. Carefully invert the cakes onto a rack and let them cool at room temperature.

For the filling, in the bowl of a stand mixer fitted with the paddle attachment, combine the ricotta, mascarpone, and icing sugar and beat on medium just until combined; don't overmix the filling or the mascarpone will separate and become too wet. Add the mini chocolate

→

→

chips and use a wooden spoon or rubber spatula to fold them into the filling. Transfer the filling to a bowl, cover, and refrigerate until set, about 1 hour.

For the frosting, in the bowl of a stand mixer fitted with the paddle attachment (no need to wash the bowl and paddle this time), combine the mascarpone and icing sugar and beat on high until combined. I warn you that this is very tricky step: Be careful to not overmix the mascarpone or it will separate and become too wet. Cover the frosting and refrigerate it until ready to use.

To assemble the cake, place one cake layer on a cake stand, serving plate, or turntable and use a rubber spatula to spread the filling on top. Place the second cake layer on top. Use an off-set spatula to spread the frosting over the top and the sides of the cake, reserving a little frosting for decorating. Decorate the cake by pressing mini chocolate chips on the sides of the cake. Transfer any remaining frosting to a piping bag fitted with a small pastry tip and pipe rosettes on top of the cake. Dust the rosettes with cinnamon then cut the cake into slices and serve. This cake can be stored in the refrigerator for up to 3 days.

Fette al limone

LEMON BARS

INGREDIENTS
Makes about 12 bars

For the crust

- 280 g (2 cups) plain flour (all-purpose flour)
- 226 g (1 cup) unsalted butter, at room temperature
- 100 g (½ cup) granulated sugar
- ½ teaspoon pure vanilla extract or paste (or the seeds of ½ vanilla bean pod)
- ¼ teaspoon fine salt

For the filling

- 600 g (3 cups) granulated sugar
- 145 g (1 cup plus ½ tablespoon) plain flour (all-purpose flour)
- 3 tablespoons potato starch
- 6 large organic eggs
- Zest of 5 or 6 organic lemons
- 250 ml (1 cup plus 2 teaspoons) freshly squeezed lemon juice

Tangy, bright, sweet, and addictive for those who love lemons! You can play around and substitute lemons for oranges or why not...Also limes! But you will need more juice if you wants to try this recipe, using limes. Picnic anyone?

METHOD For the crust, preheat the oven to 180°C (350°F). Grease a 21.5 cm (8½ inch) square cake pan then line the bottom with parchment paper.

In a large bowl, combine the plain flour, butter, granulated sugar, vanilla, and salt then use your hands to knead the ingredients together to form a dough. Press the dough evenly into the bottom of the prepared pan and bake for 15 to 20 minutes, or until golden. Place the pan on a rack and let the crust cool at room temperature while you make the filling. Leave the oven on.

For the filling, in a large bowl, combine the granulated sugar, plain flour, potato starch, eggs, and lemon zest and juice. Whisk to combine. Pour the filling over the still warm crust and bake for 20 minutes, or until the filling is set but still jiggles if you shake the pan. Place the pan on a rack and let the lemon bars cool completely at room temperature then refrigerate until the filling is completely set, at least 1 hour. Invert the pan onto a plate then invert it again onto a cutting board so the crust is on the bottom. Cut into squares and enjoy. The Lemon Bars can be stored in an airtight container in the refrigerator for up to 2 days.

Torta al pistacchio e cioccolato

PISTACHIO AND CHOCOLATE CAKE

INGREDIENTS

**Makes 1 cake
(21.5 cm / 8½ inch)**

Makes about 8 servings

For the cake

- 250 g (1¾ cup plus ½ tablespoon) plain flour (all-purpose flour)
- 1 tablespoon baking powder
- Pinch of fine salt
- 5 large organic eggs
- 250 g (1¼ cups) granulated sugar
- 256 g (1 cup plus 2 tablespoons) unsalted butter, melted and cooled to room temperature
- 1 teaspoon orange blossom honey
- 1 teaspoon pure vanilla extract or paste (or the seeds of 1 vanilla bean pod)
- 100 g (⅔ cup plus 1 tablespoon) shelled pistachios, roughly chopped

For the chocolate ganache

- 350 g (12¼ ounces) dark chocolate, at least 55% cacao
- 300 ml (1¼ cups) double whipping cream (heavy cream)
- 2 tablespoons plus 1 teaspoon unsalted butter
- 3 tablespoons glucose syrup or light corn syrup

Rustic cakes—don't you love them? I do! They talk to me about the past and the traditions of a place. They also make me feel at home and they are so much fun to make. Anyone can feel like an expert while making rustic cakes, but don't be fooled. They still require a certain amount of technique and concentration. Pistachio and chocolate—what is there to say? These two ingredients are made for each other. I usually keep my decorations very simple—that's just how I like it—but feel free to decorate this cake as you like.

METHOD For the cake, preheat the oven to 170°C (335°F). Grease a 21.5 cm (8½ inch) springform pan. Set a rack inside a baking sheet.

Sift the plain flour into a medium bowl then add the baking powder and salt and whisk to combine.

In the bowl of a stand mixer fitted with the whisk attachment or in a large bowl if using an electric mixer, combine the eggs and granulated sugar and whip until light and very pale. With the mixer on low, gradually start adding the melted and cooled butter in a slow, steady stream and beat until fully incorporated. Add the orange blossom honey and vanilla and whisk to combine. Add the flour mixture and use a wooden spoon or spatula to gently fold just until the flour is incorporated. Add the pistachios and briefly stir to combine. Pour the batter into the prepared pan and bake for 40 to 45 minutes, or until a wooden pick inserted in the centre of the cake comes out clean. Place the pan on a rack, release the cake from the pan and let it cool completely.

When the cake is completely cooled, start making the chocolate ganache. Chop the chocolate as finely as possible to ensure it melts evenly.

In a medium saucepan, bring the double whipping cream, butter, and glucose syrup to a boil. Remove the pan from the heat, add the chopped chocolate, and stir until completely melted. Let cool for 10 minutes at room temperature.

Transfer the slightly cooled ganache to a jug for easier handling then pour it over the cake, gently shaking the baking sheet to allow the ganache to drip and cover the cake properly. Let the cake stand at room temperature to set. Decorate if desired then cut into slices and serve.

Torta al caffè

ESPRESSO COFFEE CAKE

INGREDIENTS

Makes 1 cake
(21.5 cm / 8½ inch)
Makes about 8 servings

- 140 g (1 cup) plain flour
  (all-purpose flour)
- 20 g (¼ cup) unsweetened
  cocoa powder
- 2 teaspoons
  espresso powder
- 1½ teaspoons
  baking powder
- Pinch of fine salt
- 5 large organic eggs,
  at room temperature
- 165 g (3/4 cup plus 1½
  tablespoons)
  granulated sugar
- 80 ml (⅓ cup) strong
  brewed espresso, hot
- 2 teaspoons pure vanilla
  extract or paste (or the
  seeds of 2 vanilla bean pods)
- 60 g (¼ cup plus 1 teaspoon)
  unsalted butter, melted and
  cooled to room temperature

For decorating

- 250 ml (1 cup plus
  2 teaspoons) double
  whipping cream
  (heavy cream)
- 2 teaspoons strong
  brewed espresso, chilled
- Cocoa beans or chocolate
  covered coffee beans
  (optional)

This is a real coffee cake, the kind you find in coffee shops around the world. You can use this recipe as a template for countless variations. For example, you can add chocolate chips or nuts, frost it with a coffee mascarpone cream (instead of the coffee whipped cream used here), or drizzle freshly brewed coffee all over the cake and serve it warm with a dollop of vanilla ice cream. The possibilities are endless! I like to share recipes that you can change and make your own, so have fun creating!

METHOD Preheat the oven to 175°C (335°F). Grease a 21.5 cm (8½ inch) springform pan then line the bottom with parchment paper.

Sift the plain flour into a medium bowl then add the cocoa powder, espresso powder, baking powder, and salt and whisk to combine.

In the bowl of a stand mixer fitted with the whisk attachment, or in a large bowl if using an electric mixer, combine the eggs and granulated sugar and whip until light and very pale then add the hot brewed espresso and vanilla and whisk to incorporate. With the mixer on low, gradually add the melted and cooled butter in a slow, steady stream and beat until fully incorporated. Add the flour mixture in three additions and beat just until fully incorporated, being careful to not overbeat the batter. Pour the batter into the prepared pan and bake for 45 to 50 minutes, or until a wooden pick inserted in the centre comes out clean. Place the pan on a rack and let the cake cool at room temperature then release and remove the sides of the pan and transfer the cake to a cake stand or a serving plate.

To decorate the cake, in the bowl of a stand mixer fitted with the whisk attachment, combine the double whipping cream and chilled brewed espresso and whip until stiff peaks form. Using a rubber spatula, spread the coffee whipped cream all over the top of the cake. Decorate with cocoa beans or chocolate covered coffee beans, if desired, then cut the cake into slices and serve. This cake can be stored in the refrigerator for up to 2 days.

Torta di compleanno alle ciliegie e mandorle

CHERRY AND ALMOND BIRTHDAY CAKE

INGREDIENTS

Makes 1 (20 cm / 8 inch) cake
Makes about 12 servings

For the cake

- 330 g (2¼ cups plus 2 tablespoons) plain flour (all-purpose flour)
- 1 tablespoon baking powder
- Pinch of fine salt
- 168 g (¾ cup) unsalted butter, at room temperature
- 300 g (1½ cups) granulated sugar
- 180 g (¾ cup) full-fat plain Greek yogurt, at room temperature
- 1½ teaspoons natural almond extract
- 1 teaspoon pure vanilla extract or paste (or the seeds of 1 vanilla bean pod)
- 6 large organic egg whites, at room temperature
- 240 ml (1 cup) whole milk, at room temperature

For the Swiss meringue cherry buttercream frosting

- 450 g (2¼ cups) granulated sugar
- 225 ml (¾ cup plus 3 tablespoons) water
- 8 large organic egg whites
- Pinch of fine salt
- 650 g (2¾ cups plus 2 tablespoons) unsalted butter, at room temperature
- 2 teaspoons pure vanilla extract or paste (or the seeds of 1 vanilla bean pod)
- 100 g (½ cup) chopped maraschino cherries, plus 2 teaspoons maraschino cherry juice

For decorating

- Cherry jam
- Maraschino cherries

NOTE All the ingredients must be at room temperature!

I have always believed that birthday cakes should have that vintage flair. Don't you agree? They should be tall, delicious, and classic, and this cake has it all! It's a little time-consuming to make, but it is well worth it. After all, you are making this cake for a special person, right?

METHOD For the cake, preheat the oven to 170°C (335°F). Grease three shallow or two standard 20 cm (8 inch) round cake pans then line the bottoms with parchment paper.

Sift the plain flour into a medium bowl then add the baking powder and salt and whisk to combine.

In the bowl of a stand mixer fitted with the paddle attachment, beat the butter and granulated sugar until pale and fluffy. Add the yogurt, almond extract, and vanilla and beat to incorporate. Add the egg whites in two additions and beat until combined. With the mixer on low, add the flour mixture in three additions, alternating with the milk. Turn the mixer to medium-high and beat just until combined, being careful to not overbeat the batter. Divide the batter evenly between the prepared pans and bake for about 25 minutes if using three shallow pans or about 40 minutes, if using two standard pans, or until a wooden pick inserted in the centre of each cake comes out clean. Place the pans on a rack and let the cakes cool completely.

For the Swiss meringue cherry buttercream frosting, in a medium saucepan, bring the granulated sugar and water to a boil over medium heat.

While the sugar syrup is coming to a boil, in the bowl of stand mixer fitted with the whisk attachment, combine the egg whites and salt.

→

→

Use a thermometer to check the temperature of the sugar syrup. When it reaches 115°C (239°F), start whipping the egg whites on high. When the egg whites form soft peaks, remove the sugar syrup from the heat and turn the mixer to low. Very carefully pour the hot sugar syrup into the whipping egg whites and beat until the bowl is cool to the touch. Once the meringue is cool, add the butter, vanilla, and cherry juice and whip until firm. Don't panic if the texture is too loose at first; keep beating and it will come together. It is a matter of temperatures here, so make sure the meringue is NOT hot when you add the butter. Once the butter, vanilla and cherry juice are added, beat for about 15 minutes. Place the buttercream in the fridge to set for at least 30 minutes.

To assemble the cake, place one cake layer on a cake board or serving plate and spread a little cherry jam over the entire surface. Use a rubber spatula to spread the frosting on top then sprinkle with some chopped cherries. Place a second cake layer on top of the frosting and repeat the previous steps. (If making a three-layer cake, repeat this process a third time.) Using an off-set spatula, cover the top and sides of the cake with the remaining frosting. If you have leftover frosting, you can transfer it to a piping bag fitted with a medium star or round pastry tip and pipe rosettes all around the cake and then top them with more maraschino cherries. This cake can be stored in the refrigerator for up to 2 days.

Torta meringata

MERINGUE CAKE

INGREDIENTS

Makes 1 (20 cm / 8 inch) cake
Makes about 8 servings

For the meringue
- 7 large organic pasteurized egg whites
- 200 g (1 cup) granulated sugar
- 200 g (1⅔ cups) icing sugar (confectioners' sugar)

For the filling
- 500 ml (2 cups plus 1 tablespoon) double whipping cream (heavy cream)
- 70 g (½ cup plus 1 tablespoon) icing sugar (confectioners' sugar)
- 1 teaspoon pure vanilla extract or paste (or the seeds of 1 vanilla bean pod)
- 250 g (8¾ ounces) wild strawberries (or any fruit you like)

NOTE I strongly recommend using a stand mixture or an electric mixer for this recipe.

The meringue cake was born in 1720 in Meiringen, Switzerland. Many books talk about the ways each country has changed the original recipe, but the real torta meringata consists of very few ingredients, just egg whites, sugar, and cream. If you wish to stick to the original, there are no added colours or fancy ingredients. Keep it simple and simply enjoy it!

METHOD For the meringue, preheat the oven to 120°C (250°F). On a large sheet of parchment paper, use a pencil and a 20 cm (8 inch) round cake pan to trace two circles side by side. Flip the parchment paper over so the pencil marks don't show then place the parchment paper on a baking sheet. Fit a piping bag with a medium round pastry tip.

In a bowl of a stand mixer fitted with the whisk attachment, whip the egg whites and 100 g (½ cup) of the granulated sugar on medium for a few minutes then add the remaining granulated sugar and whip on high until stiff peaks form. With the mixer on low, gradually add the icing sugar. When all the icing sugar has been added, turn the mixer to high and whip until fully combined.

Transfer the meringue to the prepared piping bag and using the pencil-drawn circles as your guide, pipe 2 circles, measuring at least 2.5 cm (1 inch) in height. Continue piping meringue to fill in both circles completely. These will be the base and the top of the cake. With the remaining meringue, pipe small and medium spikes onto the parchment paper. These will be for decoration. Bake for about 1½ hours, or until crispy on top but not burnt then turn the oven off but leave the meringues in the oven with the door slightly open overnight.

→

The next day, remove the meringues from the oven. Fit a piping bag with a medium round pastry tip.

For the filling, in the bowl of a stand mixer fitted with the whisk attachment, whip 250 ml (1 cup plus 2 teaspoons) of the double whipping cream on medium until medium-stiff peaks form. Add 35 g (¼ cup plus ½ tablespoon) of the icing sugar and the vanilla and whip until stiff peaks form. Transfer the whipped cream to the prepared piping bag.

Place one meringue cake layer inside a 20 cm (8 inch) pastry ring or springform pan. Pipe some whipped cream around the meringue, filling the space between the meringue and the pastry ring or springform pan. Pipe some whipped cream on top of the meringue and use a rubber spatula to make it an even layer. Top with strawberries, reserving some for the decoration. Add a little more cream, then place the other meringue cake layer on top. Place the cake in the freezer for at least 4 hours.

Before removing the cake from the freezer, whip the remaining cream to a medium stiff consistency and use it to frost and decorate the cake: Remove the cake from the pastry ring or release and remove the sides of the springform pan. Using a rubber spatula, frost the top and sides of the cake with the freshly whipped cream. Crumble the medium meringue spikes with your hands then press them onto the sides of the cake. Use the small meringue spikes and the remaining strawberries to decorate the top of the cake. Place the cake in the freezer to set, removing it about 30 minutes before serving. This cake can be wrapped and frozen for up to 1 month or stored in the refrigerator for up to 1 day.

Boston Cream Pie

INGREDIENTS

Makes 1 (20 cm / 8 inch) cake
Makes about 12 servings

For the pastry cream

- 5 large organic egg yolks
- 200 g (1 cup) granulated sugar
- 40 g (¼ cup) cornstarch, preferably organic
- 500 ml (2 cups plus 1 tablespoon) whole milk
- 1 tablespoon unsalted butter, cold and cut into small pieces
- 2 teaspoons pure vanilla extract or paste (or the seeds from 2 vanilla bean pods)

For the cake

- 340 g (2¼ cups plus 3 tablespoons) plain flour (all-purpose flour)
- 1 tablespoon baking powder
- Pinch of fine salt
- 168 g (¾ cup) unsalted butter, at room temperature
- 300 g (1½ cups) granulated sugar
- 5 large organic eggs
- 2 teaspoons pure vanilla extract or paste (or the seeds of 1 vanilla bean pod)
- 300 ml (1¼ cups) whole milk, at room temperature

For the chocolate ganache

- 150 ml (½ cup plus 2 tablespoons) double whipping cream (heavy cream)
- 2 tablespoons glucose syrup or light corn syrup
- 200 g (7 ounces) dark chocolate, preferably 55% cacao, roughly chopped

Boston Cream Pie, Massachusetts's official state dessert, isn't a pie, and it's not well known why it's called a pie. A proper vanilla sponge cake, filled with pastry cream and topped with chocolate ganache, Boston Cream Pie is easy and simple but amazingly good! Allow the cakes to fully cool before filling with pastry cream and chill the cake before pouring the ganache over top. You also need to prepare the pastry cream the day before. Trust me: These tips will make it easier to assemble the cake.

METHOD For the pastry cream, in a medium bowl, quickly whisk the egg yolks.

In a large saucepan, combine the granulated sugar, cornstarch, and milk and bring to a gentle boil, stirring constantly, over medium heat. Temper the egg yolks by slowly pouring a little of the milk mixture into the bowl and whisking quickly. Pour the egg mixture into the saucepan, place over medium heat, and cook, whisking constantly, until thick, about 2 minutes. Remove from the heat, add the butter and vanilla, and stir to incorporate. Pour the pastry cream into a large bowl, cover with plastic wrap, pressing the plastic onto the surface of the cream to prevent a skin from forming, and refrigerate overnight.

For the sponge cakes, preheat the oven to 170°C (335°F). Grease two 20 cm (8 inch) round cake pans then line the bottoms with parchment paper.

Sift the plain flour into a large bowl. Add the baking powder and salt and whisk to combine.

In the bowl of a stand mixer fitted with the paddle attachment, beat the butter and granulated sugar on high until very pale and fluffy. Add the eggs, one at a time, followed by the vanilla, and beat until fully incorporated. Scrape down the sides of the bowl then add the flour

→

mixture in three additions, alternating with the milk. Divide the batter between the prepared pans and bake for 25 to 30 minutes, or until a toothpick inserted in the centre of each cake comes out almost clean. Be careful to not overbake this cake. Carefully invert the cakes onto a rack and let cool completely at room temperature. If either cake has developed a dome shape, use a serrated knife to trim the excess and make it flat.

Place 1 cake layer on a cake stand or serving plate. Remove the pastry cream from the fridge and give it a stir. Use a rubber spatula to spread the pastry cream evenly on top of the cake layer then place the second cake layer on top. Refrigerate the cake while you prepare the ganache.

For the ganache, in a medium saucepan, bring the double whipping cream and glucose syrup to a gentle boil over low heat. Remove from the heat, add the chopped chocolate, and stir until completely melted. Let cool for no more than 5 minutes.

Remove the cake from the fridge and pour the ganache over the top, allowing it to drip down the sides. Place the cake back in the fridge to set, removing it about 20 minutes before serving. This cake can be stored in the refrigerator for up to 3 days.

Torta al cioccolato 1000 strati

THOUSAND LAYER CHOCOLATE CAKE

INGREDIENTS

Makes 1 very tall 21.5 cm (8½ inch) cake

For the chocolate pastry cream

- 540 ml (2¼ cups plus 1 teaspoon) whole milk
- 200 ml (¾ cup plus 4 teaspoons) double whipping cream (heavy cream)
- 140 g (⅔ cup plus 2 teaspoons) granulated sugar
- Pinch of fine salt
- 6 large organic egg yolks
- 40 g (¼ cup) cornstarch, preferably organic
- 120 g (4¼ ounces) dark chocolate, at least 55% cacao, finely chopped
- 60 g (¼ cup plus 1 teaspoon) unsalted butter, cold and cut into small pieces
- 2 teaspoons pure vanilla extract or paste (or the seeds of 2 vanilla bean pods)

For the vanilla simple syrup

- 200 g (1 cup) granulated sugar
- 200 ml (¾ cup plus 4 teaspoons) water
- 1 teaspoons pure vanilla extract or paste (or the seeds of 1 vanilla bean pod)

For the cake

- 385 g (2¾ cups) plain flour (all-purpose flour)
- 1 teaspoon baking powder
- 1 teaspoon baking soda
- ½ teaspoon fine salt
- 340 g (1½ cups) unsalted butter, at room temperature
- 400 g (2 cups) granulated sugar
- 5 large organic eggs
- 2 tablespoons vegetable oil, preferably non-GMO (or sunflower oil)
- 2 tsp pure vanilla extract or paste (or the seeds of two pods)
- 180 ml (¾ cup) fresh brewed coffee, hot
- 70 g (¾ cup plus 2 tablespoons) unsweetened cocoa powder
- 240 g (1 cup) sour cream or full-fat Greek yogurt, at room temperature

For the ganache

- 660 ml (2¾ cups) double whipping cream (heavy cream)
- 590 g (20¾ ounces) dark chocolate, at least 55% cacao, finely chopped

When I was in New York City in 2013, I heard about a place called Strip House and their legendary 24-layer chocolate cake. A cake that defies gravity! With 24 decadent chocolate cake layers filled with chocolate pastry cream and covered with chocolate ganache, it's not surprising that many people cannot finish a slice. Could I miss it? No way! Challenge accepted! I headed to Strip House, only to discover it's a steak house. Me and steak are not a good match—I'm vegetarian—but I decided to order a slice of cake anyway. I had to try it. The waiter delivered a gigantic slice of cake, along with a gigantic glass of ice water—only later, would I understand the reason for the huge glass of water. Bravely, I dug in my fork, starting from the top and allowing it to sink into the cake until it hit the bottom, and.... OMG!!!! I was in cake heaven! With the help of my glass of water, I finished the whole thing! It was a matter of principle, but also a matter of pride. I never leave food on my plate, and I certainly never leave cake! I would rather fast for three days, than throw away a piece of cake.

I was lucky enough to get a few tips from Strip House's pastry chef and created my own version. It's a lot of work, but the final result will cause friends and family to keep you in their hearts forever, and possibly show up at your door, unannounced and in search of a slice! To make the process a bit easier, bake the cake layers up to two days ahead, wrap them in plastic wrap, and store them in the fridge. It will be easier to slice them if you're not an expert. I also recommend making the chocolate pastry cream and vanilla simple syrup one day ahead. Otherwise, be patient, follow the recipe carefully, and be proud of yourself for making it!

METHOD For the chocolate pastry cream, in a medium saucepan, bring the milk, double whipping cream, 100 g (½ cup) of the granulated sugar, and the salt to a simmer over medium heat, stirring to dissolve the sugar and salt.

In a medium bowl, whisk the egg yolks with the remaining granulated sugar. Add the cornstarch and whisk to combine.

Temper the eggs by slowly pouring a little of the milk mixture into the bowl and whisking quickly. Pour the egg mixture into the saucepan, place over medium heat, and cook, whisking constantly, until thick. Remove from the heat then add the chocolate, butter, and vanilla and stir until melted. Strain the pastry cream through a fine-mesh sieve set over a medium bowl. Cover with plastic wrap, pressing the plastic onto the surface of the cream to prevent a skin from forming, and refrigerate until ready to use.

For the vanilla syrup, in a small saucepan, bring the granulated sugar, water, and vanilla to a boil. Remove from the heat and let cool at room temperature until ready to use or refrigerate if making ahead.

For the cake, preheat the oven to 170°C (335°F). Grease two 21.5 cm (8½ inch) springform pans then line the bottoms with parchment paper.

Sift the plain flour into a medium bowl. Add the baking soda, baking

→

powder, and salt and whisk to combine. In the bowl of a stand mixer fitted with the paddle attachment, beat the butter and granulated sugar until pale and fluffy. With the mixer on low, add the eggs, one at a time, followed by the vegetable oil and vanilla, and beat until fully combined.

In a large bowl, whisk together the hot coffee and cocoa powder. With the mixer on low, add the coffee mixture to the batter. Add the flour mixture in three batches, alternating with the sour cream and scraping down the bowl as needed. Divide the batter between the prepared pans and bake for 35 to 40 minutes, or until a toothpick inserted in the centre of each cake comes out clean. Place the pans on a rack and let the cakes cool for at least 30 minutes then release and remove the sides of the pan and let the cakes cool completely at room temperature.

Preheat the oven to 170°C (335°F). Line a baking sheet with parchment paper. Place a 21.5 or 24 (8½ to 9½ inch) cm cardboard cake round in the bottom of each springform pan.

Place one cake layer on a cutting board. Use a serrated knife to trim the dome from the top of the cake and make it flat. Reserve the cake trimmings for decorating. Cut the cake crosswise into six thin layers. The cake layers are very fragile, so be careful not to break them. Repeat the same process with the second cake layer. You will have 12 thin layers in total.

Place each thin cake layer on a sheet of parchment paper. Using a pastry brush, brush the vanilla simple syrup over each cake layer.

Use your hands to crumble the cake trimmings onto the prepared baking sheet. Bake for 8 to 10 minutes. Place the sheet on a rack and let the crumbles cool.

Place one of the thicker cake layers on the cardboard inside one of the spring-

form pans. Use a rubber spatula to spread an even layer of chocolate pastry cream on top. Repeat this process five more times, finishing with a final layer of chocolate pastry cream. Repeat this process with the other springform pan, using the remaining cake layers and the remaining chocolate pastry cream, but this time, finish with a cake layer rather than chocolate pastry cream. You will end up with two 12-layer cakes for a total of 24 layers. Place both cakes in the freezer to set for about 1 hour.

For the chocolate ganache, in a large saucepan, bring the double whipping cream to a simmer over medium heat. Remove from the heat, add the chopped chocolate, and stir until fully melted. Let cool no more than 5 minutes.

When the cakes have chilled, remove the one with the cake on top from the freezer. Pour some ganache over the top of the cake and gently tilt the pan to spread the ganache and cover the entire top. Place cake back in the freezer to set for another hour.

When the cakes have chilled again, remove them from the freezer. Carefully, remove the sides of the springform pans. (If needed, use a blowtorch or blow-dryer to warm the sides of the pan and release the cake.)

Place the bottom half of the cake (the one with chocolate pastry cream on top) on a cake stand or serving plate. Use a blowtorch or blow-dryer over the entire cake to slightly soften the chocolate pastry cream so that the top layer will attach itself easier. Carefully place the top half of the cake on the bottom half. Using an off-set spatula, spread the softened chocolate pastry cream that's already on the cake into an even layer. Press the chocolate cake crumbles onto the sides of the cake. If you made it to this step, you made it through!!! GOOD JOB! Here you have your majestic chocolate cake!

Biscotti krumiri

KRUMIRI COOKIES

INGREDIENTS
Makes about 40 cookies

- 140 (⅔ cup plus 2 teaspoons) granulated sugar
- 120 g (½ cup plus 1 teaspoon) unsalted butter, at room temperature
- 1 large organic egg plus 2 large organic egg yolks
- 1 tablespoon honey
- 1 teaspoon pure vanilla extract or paste (or the seeds of 1 vanilla bean pod)
- Pinch of fine salt
- 350 g (3 cups) 00 flour

NOTE I use a stand mixer to make these cookies, but you can mix the dough by hand.

These cookies originated in Piedmont, in a town called Casale Monferrato, in 1878, the year King Vittorio Emanuele II died. They were created by pastry chef Domenico Rossi as a tribute to the king and are said to resemble his king's moustache.

The name krumiri came up during the demonstrations for workers' rights in early 1900. It's believed that the word krumiri comes from crumiro, which means "the one who doesn't participate in a strike" but in the Northern dialect, krumiri also derives from Khumir, the name of the belligerent Tunisian tribe that caused the French invasion of Tunis in 1881.

The internet is full of recipes claiming to be the "original", but no one can claim to know the real recipe. The only thing one can do is eat these cookies and try to make the closest possible version, and that's what I did. I hope you enjoy my krumiri cookies, but above all, I hope you visit Casale Monferrato to get the real deal!

METHOD Preheat the oven to 190°C (375°C). Line a baking sheet with parchment paper. Fit a piping bag with a medium star pastry tip.

In the bowl of a stand mixer fitted with the paddle attachment, beat the granulated sugar and butter until pale and fluffy. Add the whole egg and egg yolks, one at a time, followed by the honey, vanilla, and salt and beat until incorporated. Sift the 00 flour into the bowl in small additions and mix until just combined, being careful not to overmix the dough. Transfer the dough to the prepared piping bag and pipe it into slightly curved logs, measuring about 5 cm (2 inches) or smaller, onto to the prepared baking sheet. Bake for about 20 minutes, or until golden. Place the baking sheet on a rack and let the cookies cool completely before touching them. Krumiri cookies will keep in an airtight container at room temperature for about 2 weeks.

Torta di primavera

A CAKE FOR SPRING

INGREDIENTS

Makes 1 (20 cm / 8 inch) cake

Makes about 8 to 10 servings

For the simple syrup

- 150 g (¾ cup) granulated sugar
- 150 ml (½ cup plus 2 tablespoons) water
- Juice of 1 organic lemon
- Juice of 1 organic orange
- 2 teaspoons pure vanilla extract or paste (or the seeds of 2 vanilla bean pods)

For the cake

- 150 g (1¼ cups) 00 flour
- 150 g (1 cup plus 3 tablespoons) almond flour
- 1½ teaspoons baking powder
- 150 g (⅔ cup) unsalted butter, at room temperature
- 130 g (⅔ cup) granulated sugar
- 1 teaspoon pure vanilla extract or paste (or the seeds of 1 vanilla bean pod)
- 5 large organic eggs
- 2 tablespoons whole milk

For the chantilly cream

- 500 ml (2 cups plus 1 tablespoon) double whipping cream (heavy cream)
- 80 g (⅔ cup) icing sugar (confectioners' sugar)
- 1 teaspoon pure vanilla extract or paste (or the seeds of 1 vanilla bean pod)

For decorating

- 500 g (17½ ounces) fresh organic strawberries
- 100 g (1 cup) sliced almonds
- some white chocolate, sliced into long shavings

To me, nothing says "spring" more than strawberries and cream! Don't you agree? I also strongly believe that this recipe cannot be excluded from your personal recipe repertoire. It's one of those recipes that one should always have on hand to impress, delight, and enjoy! This cake is lovely for birthdays, brunches, and picnics. Imagine how pretty it looks served on a plate sitting on a beautiful blanket or tablecloth. Looking for a perfect picture? Look no further; this cake is for you!

METHOD For the simple syrup, in a medium saucepan, bring the granulated sugar, water, lemon juice, orange juice, and vanilla to a boil over medium heat, stirring to completely dissolve the sugar. Let cool completely at room temperature before using. The simple syrup can be made ahead and refrigerated in an airtight container for up to 1 week.

For the cake, preheat the oven to 170°C (335°F). Grease two 20 cm (8 inch) round cakes then line the bottoms with parchment paper.

Sift the 00 flour, almond flour, and baking powder into a medium bowl.

In the bowl of a stand mixer fitted with the paddle attachment, beat the butter and granulated sugar until very pale and fluffy. Add the vanilla. With the mixer on low, add the eggs, one at a time, and beat until incorporated. Add the flour mixture in three additions, alternating with the milk; be careful to not overmix the batter. Divide the batter between

→

the prepared pans and bake for 30 to 40 minutes, or until a wooden pick inserted in the centre of each cake comes out clean. Place the pans on a rack and let the cakes cool at room temperature.

For the chantilly cream, in the bowl of a stand mixer fitted with the whisk attachment, whip the double whipping cream and icing sugar until medium-stiff peaks form. Add the vanilla and whip until stiff peaks form.

Place one cake layer on a cake board, cake stand, or cake plate. Using a long, serrated knife, trim the top of the cake to remove the top. Pour the simple syrup all over the surface of the cake. (I want my cakes to be very juicy, so I use a lot of syrup, but if you like a drier cake, only use half the amount.) Use a rubber spatula to spread a dollop of chantilly cream on top of the cake. Arrange some strawberries in the chantilly cream. Place the second cake layer on top then use the spatula to spread the remaining chantilly cream on the top and sides of the cake. If you have leftover chantilly cream and like to pipe, add rosettes around the top. Gently press the sliced almonds onto the sides of the cake. Cut any remaining strawberries and arrange them in the centre as well as the white chocolate shavings to finish the cake. Cut into slices and serve. This cake can be stored in the refrigerator for up to 2 days.

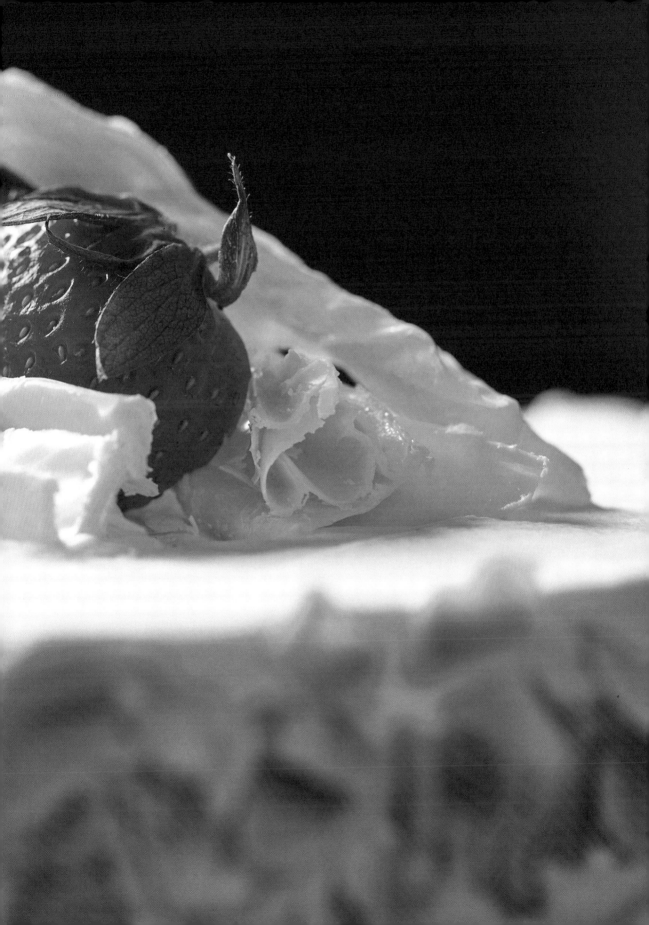

Loaf marmorizzato al tè matcha e cocco

MATCHA AND COCONUT MARBLE POUND CAKE

INGREDIENTS

**Makes 1 loaf cake
(21.5 cm / 8½ inch)**
Makes about 8 to 10 servings

For the cake

· 240 g (1⅔ cups plus
  1 tablespoon) plain flour
  (all-purpose flour)
· 1½ teaspoons
  baking powder
· 240 g (1 cup plus 1
  tablespoon) unsalted butter,
  at room temperature
· 240 g (1 cup plus
  2 tablespoons plus 2
  teaspoons) granulated sugar
· 240 g (8½ ounces) organic
  eggs (about 4 large eggs)
· 2 teaspoons pure vanilla
  extract or paste (or the
  seeds of 2 vanilla bean pods)
· 60 ml (¼ cup) full-fat
  coconut milk
· 2 tablespoons matcha tea
  powder

For the frosting

· 150 g (⅔ cup) unsalted
  butter, at room temperature
· 370 g (3 cups plus
  1 tablespoon) icing sugar
  (confectioners' sugar)
· About 60 ml (¼ cup)
  full-fat coconut milk, cold

For decorating

· Shaved coconut

Coconut is one of those ingredients that people tend to either love or hate. I happen to love it. I am not, however, a big fan of matcha tea, but guess what? I love this recipe! While I don't like drinking it, I discovered that I can enjoy the best of matcha tea if I use it in a cake. And this marble pound cake is truly delicious. There's a lesson here: If you are suspicious of coconut, matcha, or any ingredient, consider trying it in a different form. Let me know what you think...you know how to find me.

METHOD For the cake, preheat the oven to 170°C (335°F). Grease a 21.5 cm (8½ inch) loaf pan then line it with parchment paper.

Sift the plain flour into a large bowl. Add the baking powder and whisk to combine.

In the bowl of a stand mixer fitted with the paddle attachment, beat the butter and granulated sugar until very pale and fluffy.

In a small bowl, quickly whisk the eggs. With the mixer on low, add the eggs, followed by the vanilla, and beat until fully incorporated. Add the flour mixture in three additions, alternating with the coconut milk, and beat until just combined. Divide the batter evenly between two bowls. Add the matcha powder to one bowl and whisk until fully incorporated.

Place a spoonful of the plain cake batter in a corner of the prepared pan then place a spoonful of the matcha cake batter next to it. Repeat until you cover the entire bottom of the pan then continue adding alternating spoonfuls of the plain and matcha batters until you run out of batter. Swirl a long wooden pick in the pan to roughly marble the two batters. Bake for about 1 hour, or until a wooden pick inserted in the centre comes out clean. Place the pan on a rack and let the cake cool completely. (At this point, the cake can be wrapped in plastic wrap and frozen for up to 3 months.)

For the frosting, in the bowl of a stand mixer fitted with the paddle attachment, or in a large bowl if using an electric mixer, beat the butter and icing sugar until creamy. Add the cold coconut milk and gently beat on low until creamy and fluffy.

When the cake is completely cool, remove it from the pan and place it on a serving tray. Use an off-set or rubber spatula to spread the frosting all over the top of the cake. Sprinkle some shaved coconut on top and serve.

Bakewell tart for my friend Leila

INGREDIENTS

Makes 1 (23 cm / 9 inch) tart
Makes about 8 to 10 servings

For the pastry dough

· 200 g (1¼ cups plus
  3 tablespoons) plain flour
  (all-purpose flour)
· 2½ tablespoons icing sugar
  (confectioners' sugar)
· Pinch of fine salt
· 110 g (7 tablespoons plus
  2 teaspoons) unsalted
  butter, cold and cut into
  small pieces
· 1 large organic egg
· Zest of 1 organic lemon
· 1 tablespoon ice water

For the filling

· 200 g (¾ cup plus
  2 tablespoons)
  unsalted butter
· 215 g (1 cup plus
  1 tablespoon)
  granulated sugar
· 225 g (2¼ cups)
  ground almonds
· 4 large organic eggs, beaten
· 100 g (⅓ cup) cherry jam
· 120 g (1 cup plus 2 tablespoons) sliced almonds

For the icing

· 100 g (¾ cup plus
  1 tablespoon) icing sugar
  (confectioners' sugar)

NOTE I make the pastry dough
by hand, but you can use an
electric mixer or a stand mixer
if you prefer.

Leila is my dearest friend. She is English but has lived in Italy for more than 20 years. When she told me that Bakewell tart is one of her favourite desserts, I knew I wanted to make my own version for this book and dedicate the recipe to her. Leila usually asks me to bake my chocolate layer cake for her birthday, but since there are already quite few chocolate cake recipes in my books, I decided to include her second favourite cake instead.

Bakewell tart is named for the town of Bakewell in Derbyshire, England, and it dates back to the nineteenth century. It's believed that a cook at a pub in Bakewell called The White Horse Inn was asked to make a jam tart, but instead of adding the almond paste and jam to the tart, he spread the mixture on top. The result was something close to an egg custard and was called a Bakewell pudding—it is amazing how so many of the best recipes, from all over the world, were created by mistake! How funny is that? It was only in 1900 that Bakewell pudding became a tart, when the eggy custard was replaced by Italian frangipane, creating what we now know as Bakewell tart. But we don't know who—or why—the filling changed. Perhaps it was an Italian cook working in the UK? It remains a secret, but one thing is for sure: This tart will disappear very quickly from your kitchen! Of that, I am sure!

METHOD For the pastry dough, sift the plain flour and icing sugar into a large bowl. Add the salt and whisk to combine. Add the butter and use your fingertips to rub it into the flour mixture until fine crumbs form. Add the egg, lemon zest, and ice water and briefly knead the dough to bring it together; be careful to not overwork the dough, or the butter will melt. Shape the dough into a disk, wrap it in plastic wrap, and refrigerate it for at least 1 hour.

Preheat the oven to 170°C (335°F). Grease a 23 cm (9 inch) round, fluted tart tin.

On a lightly floured work surface, use a rolling pin to roll out the pastry dough until about ½ cm (¼ inch). Carefully fit the dough and fit it into the prepared tart tin then refrigerate it for 15 minutes.

When the tart shell has chilled, place a sheet of parchment paper inside then fill it the with baking beans or rice. Bake for 12 minutes, or until lightly golden. Carefully remove the baking beans or rice and parchment paper and let the pastry shell cool. Leave the oven on.

For the filling, in a medium saucepan, melt the butter and granulated sugar over medium heat. Add the ground almonds and eggs, and cook, stirring constantly for 3 to 4 minutes to avoid cooking the eggs. Remove from the heat.

When the pastry shell has cooled slightly, spread the cherry jam evenly over the bottom then top with the frangipane. Sprinkle the sliced almonds all over the surface and bake for 25 minutes, or until lightly golden. Place the tart tin on a rack and let the tart cool completely.

For the icing, in a small bowl, whisk the icing sugar with just enough lukewarm water to create a thick but pourable icing. Drizzle the icing over the tart or cover it entirely. Let the tart set at room temperature before serving.

Torta al pistacchio e miele

PISTACHIO AND HONEY CAKE

INGREDIENTS

Makes 1 (25 cm / 10 inch) cake
Makes about 10 servings

For the cake

- 125 g (¾ cup plus 2 tablespoons) shelled pistachios, plus 60 g (½ cup) chopped pistachios for decorating
- 180 g (1¼ cups plus ½ tablespoon) plain flour (all-purpose flour)
- 1½ teaspoons baking powder
- ¼ teaspoon baking soda
- Pinch of fine salt
- 3 large organic eggs
- 230 g (1 cup plus 2 tablespoons) granulated sugar
- 226 g (1 cup) unsalted butter, melted and cooled
- Zest of 1 organic lemon
- 1 teaspoon pure vanilla extract or paste (or the seeds of 1 vanilla bean pod)
- 170 ml (⅔ cup plus 2 teaspoons) whole milk

For the frosting

- 500 ml (2 cups plus 1 tablespoon) double whipping cream (heavy cream)
- 1 tablespoon clear honey, plus more for drizzling

For decorating

- Mixed berries or your favourite fruit

Close your eyes and imagine you are on a terrace in the gorgeous town of Positano, or in Cinque Terre, or Portofino, or even in Greece—wherever you prefer. The sun is warm, and you are sitting at a pretty table dressed with a white linen tablecloth. Beautiful plates and pretty flowers decorate the table. The view is breathtaking. The breeze is lovely. You are holding a mimosa, and the bright yellow of the cocktail looks perfect next to the blue sea. On the table, there is a cake made with Italian pistachios and drizzled with the purest clear honey you have ever seen. Now, slowly open you eyes. In reality, you are probably in your kitchen, but you are about to make a cake that will transport you to that terrace, at least in your imagination, and believe me, it's worth it!

METHOD For the cake, preheat the oven to 170°C (335°F). Line a baking sheet with parchment paper. Grease a 25 cm (10 inch) springform pan.

Spread the whole shelled pistachios on the prepared baking sheet and bake for 8 to 10 minutes, or until crunchy, being careful to not burn the nuts. Let the pistachios cool; leave the oven on.

When the pistachios are completely cool, blend them in a food processor or blender until they resemble a fine flour.

Sift the plain flour into a large bowl. Add the baking powder, baking soda, salt, and the pistachio flour and whisk to combine.

In the bowl of a stand mixer fitted with the paddle attachment, combine the eggs and granulated sugar and beat until pale. With the mixer on low, gradually add the melted and cooled butter in a slow, steady stream. Add the lemon zest and vanilla, followed by the milk, and beat just until incorporated. Add the flour mixture and use a rubber spatula or wooden spoon to fold until just combined. Pour the batter into the prepared pan and bake for 40 minutes, or until a wooden pick inserted in the centre comes out clean. Place the pan on a rack and let the cake cool for 10 minutes then release and remove the sides of the pan and let the cake cool completely.

For the frosting, in the bowl of a stand mixer fitted with the whisk attachment, or in a large bowl if using an electric mixer, whip the double whipping cream until medium-stiff peaks form. Add the honey and whip until stiff peaks form; be careful not to overwhip the cream, or it will curdle.

Using a rubber spatula, spread the frosting over the top of the cake. Decorate with the chopped pistachios and the berries or fruit, drizzle with more honey, and serve. This cake can be stored in the refrigerator for up to 3 days.

Torta mandorle e cioccolato

ALMOND CHOCOLATE CAKE

INGREDIENTS

**Makes 1 cake
(21.5 cm / 8½ inch)
Makes about 6 to 8 servings**

For the pastry dough

- 160 g (½ cup plus 3 tablespoons) unsalted butter, at room temperature
- 130 g (⅔ cup) granulated sugar
- 1 teaspoon pure vanilla extract or paste (or the seeds of 1 vanilla bean pod)
- 1 large organic egg, plus 2 large organic egg yolks
- 330 g (2¼ cups plus 2 tablespoons) plain flour (all-purpose flour)
- Pinch of fine salt

For the filling

- 80 g (½ cup plus 1 tablespoon) plain flour (all-purpose flour)
- 20 g (¼ cup) cocoa powder
- 85 g (6 tablespoons) unsalted butter, at room temperature
- 80 g (⅔ cup plus) almond flour
- 100 g (½ cup) granulated sugar
- 1 teaspoon pure vanilla extract or paste (or the seeds of 1 vanilla bean pod)
- 2 large organic eggs

For the chocolate ganache

- 200 g (7 ounces) dark chocolate, preferably 65% cacao
- 3 tablespoons unsalted butter
- 1 tablespoon glucose syrup or honey
- Cocoa powder or icing sugar (confectioners' sugar), for dusting (optional)

Is this a tart? Hmm, yes. Is this a cake? Absolutely. Is this a triumph of different textures? It sure is! And is this one of the most decadent, rich, surprising, and elegant recipes you can make? You have my word!

METHOD For the pastry dough, in the bowl of a stand mixer fitted with the paddle attachment, combine the butter, granulated sugar, and vanilla and beat until combined. Add the whole egg and egg yolks, one at a time, and beat until incorporated. Add the plain flour and salt and beat until a dough forms. Transfer the dough to a work surface and gather it into a ball. Wrap it in plastic wrap and refrigerate for at least 1 hour and preferably overnight.

When the dough has chilled, preheat the oven to 170°C (335°F). Grease a 21.5 cm (8½ inch) springform pan then dust it with flour.

On a lightly floured work surface, use a rolling pin to roll out the dough into a round that is about 3 mm (⅛ inch) thick. Carefully lift the dough and fit it into the prepared pan. In the pan, cut the dough to about 3 cm (1¼ inch) in height. Place the tart shell in the fridge while you make the cake filling.

For the filling, sift the plain flour and cocoa powder into a large bowl.

In the bowl of a stand mixer fitted with the whisk attachment, beat the butter until pale and fluffy. Add the almond flour and granulated sugar and mix for a few seconds. Add the vanilla and eggs and beat until fully combined. Add the flour mixture and use a rubber spatula or wooden spoon to gently fold until just incorporated, being careful to not deflate the air in the batter.

Carefully spread the cake filling in the chilled tart shell and bake for about 30 minutes, or until a toothpick inserted in the centre comes out clean. Place the pan on a rack and let the cake cool for 10 minutes then release and remove the sides of the pan and let the cake cool completely at room temperature.

For the ganache, fit a piping bag with your favourite pastry tip.

Using a bain-marie, melt the chocolate. Remove from the heat then add the butter and stir until melted. Add the glucose syrup and stir to incorporate. Transfer the ganache to the prepared piping bag and pipe motifs around the edge of the cake. Allow to set for 15 minutes, then pour the rest of the ganache over the top of the cake. Refrigerate the cake until set, at least 2 hours. Serve the cake as is or dust the centre with cocoa powder or icing sugar. This cake can be stored in an airtight container at room temperature for up to 3 days.

Biscotti all'acqua di rose

ROSEWATER COOKIES

INGREDIENTS

Makes about 48 cookies

- 200 g (1¼ cups plus 3 tablespoons) plain flour (all-purpose flour)
- 50 g (6 tablespoons) almond flour
- 180 g (¾ cup plus 1 tablespoon) unsalted butter room temperature
- 1 large organic egg
- 190 g (1½ cups plus 1 tablespoon) icing sugar (confectioners' sugar), plus more for dusting
- 1½ tablespoons rosewater
- 1 teaspoon pure vanilla extract or paste (or the seeds of 1 vanilla bean pod)
- ¼ teaspoon fine salt

NOTE You can freeze the cookie dough up to 3 weeks. I recommend using an electric mixer for this recipe, because the quantities are small, but if you double or triple the recipe, use a stand mixer fitted with a paddle attachment.

Nothing is more feminine and delicate than flowers, and roses are no exception—if anything, they are the quintessential flower! You can make these cookies to celebrate spring, for a baby shower, or as a wedding favour. The recipe is very easy to scale up if you need to make a large batch and the cookies look very pretty in small bags tied with a silky ribbon. Don't ask me why, but these cookies are especially delicious with a cup of coffee! Roses and coffee? Yes, please!

METHOD Preheat the oven to 170°C (335°F). Line several baking sheets with parchment paper.

Sift the plain flour and almond flour into a medium bowl.

In a large bowl, use an electric mixer to beat the butter until pale and fluffy. Add the egg, icing sugar, rosewater, vanilla, and salt and beat just until combined. Add the flour mixture and mix on low until incorporated, being careful to not overmix the batter. Using your hands, roll the batter into 2.5 cm (1 inch) balls and arrange them on the prepared baking sheet, leaving space for the cookies to expand. If your hands are sticky, dip them in some flour. Bake for about 12 minutes, or until the cookies are lightly golden but still pale. Place the baking sheet on a rack and immediately dust the cookies with icing sugar. Let the cookies cool completely before touching or serving them. The cookies can be kept in an airtight container at room temperature for up to 5 days.

Meringhe

MERINGUES

INGREDIENTS

**Makes about
6 large meringues**

· 3 large organic egg whites,
  at room temperature
· 150 g (¾ cup) granulated
  sugar
· 1 teaspoon pure vanilla
  extract or paste (or the
  seeds of 1 vanilla bean pod)
· Pinch of fine salt
· ½ teaspoon cream of tartar
· All-natural vegetarian
  (cochineal-free) food
  colouring of your choice
· Dried fruit or chocolate
  shavings (optional)

NOTE If you prefer, you can
pipe these meringues onto the
baking sheet, but you will need
to adjust the baking time—
smaller meringues take less
time to bake.

While baking in my kitchen, I have often wondered who first decided to whisk egg whites? How did he or she come up with this concept? After a lot of research, I discovered that around 1600, an Italian pastry chef named Gasparini was the first to whip egg whites, even adding a little sugar! Of course, some food historians believe the first traces of meringue appeared in French books dating to 1692. I think whoever did this is simply a genius!

I know quite a few people love meringues. If you do, this recipe is for you. I also know that many bakers are intimidated by making meringues. If you wish to learn and become fearless, this recipe is a good place to start. It bakes in a relatively short time compared to others, so it's a good way to give meringues a go! You can flavour these meringues by adding dried fruit or chocolate shavings, but make sure any additions are completely dry, as liquid will compromise the results. I use all-natural food colouring, and I strongly recommend you do too. Actually, powdered dried fruit provides the most beautiful colours.

METHOD Preheat the oven to 120°C (250°F). Line one or more baking sheets with parchment paper.

Fill a medium saucepan with about 2.5 cm (1 inch) of water and bring to a boil over medium heat.

In the bowl of a stand mixer, combine the egg whites, granulated sugar, vanilla, and salt. Place the bowl over the saucepan, making sure the bowl doesn't touch the boiling water. Let the boiling water heat the egg white mixture, without stirring, for about 5 minutes or until the sugar is dissolved. Remove the bowl from the saucepan and fit it on the stand mixer. Using the whisk attachment, whip the egg white mixture on high until medium-stiff peaks form. Add the cream of tartar and the food colouring and whip until stiff and glossy, about 8 minutes in total. Add the dried fruit or chocolate shavings, if using, and fold them in by hand.

Using a large ice cream scoop, scoop dollops of the meringue onto the prepared baking sheet and bake for 1½ hours, or until the meringues are dry. The meringues can be kept in an airtight container at room temperature and away from any humidity for up to 3 days.

Torta mousse alla ricotta e gocce di cioccolato e fragole

RICOTTA MOUSSE CAKE WITH CHOCOLATE AND STRAWBERRIES

INGREDIENTS
Makes 1 (20 cm / 8 inch) cake
Yields 8

For the filling

- 500 g (2 cups plus 4 teaspoons) sheep's milk ricotta
- 1 teaspoon pure vanilla bean extract or paste (or the seeds of 1 vanilla bean pod)
- 500 ml (2 cups plus 1 tablespoon) double whipping cream (heavy cream)
- 140 g (1 cup plus 2 tablespoons) icing sugar (confectioners' sugar)
- 70 g (⅓ cup plus 1 tablespoon) mini chocolate chips
- 250 g (8¾ ounces) strawberries, preferably small, some chopped and some sliced

For the cake

- 250 g (8¾ ounces) organic egg whites, at room temperature, plus 360 g (12¾ ounces) organic egg yolks, at room temperature and beaten
- 250 g (1¼ cups) granulated sugar
- 250 g (1¾ cup plus ½ tablespoon) plain flour (all-purpose flour)
- Icing sugar (confectioners' sugar), for dusting

NOTE The weight of the eggs is expressed in grams this time, as it is vital to weigh the eggs for the best final result. You can use cow's milk ricotta, but sheep's milk ricotta is best for this recipe—use the best you can find. It is essential to drain the ricotta, or the mousse filling will be too runny. You can use this cake to make a cake roll (a.k.a. bisquit, roulade, Swiss roll) and for many other preparations, so keep the recipe on hand for future experiments!

I simply love this cake. Well, I love almost every cake, but I especially love this cake. It is fresh, light, and versatile, and you can play with different flavours depending on the season. When it's cold, you can add candied citrus and cinnamon, or marron glacé, orange, and chocolate, or poached pears. And when it's warm, you can play with white chocolate and all kinds of beautiful fruit—peaches, pineapple, raspberries, blackberries, cherries...you name it! This version remains my favourite!

METHOD For the filling, place the ricotta in a fine-mesh sieve set over a bowl and let it drain for at least 3 hours to release as much liquid as possible.

For the cake, preheat the oven to 220°C (425°F). Line the bottom of a 30.5 x 40.5 cm (12 x 16 inch) baking sheet with parchment paper.

In the bowl of a stand mixer fitted with the whisk attachment, whip the egg whites on low. With the machine still on low, gradually add the granulated sugar and whip until stiff peaks form then gradually add the beaten egg yolks in a slow, steady stream, mixing until fully incorporated. Turn the mixer off. Sift the plain flour into the bowl and use a rubber spatula to very gently fold it in, being careful to not deflate the batter. Gently pour the batter onto the prepared baking sheet and use an off-set spatula to spread it evenly. Bake for 5 to 6 minutes, or until the cake is pale with lightly golden edges. It's very important to not over bake this cake or it will crack. Place the baking sheet on a rack and let the cake cool completely.

Cut a sheet of parchment paper slightly larger than the cake then dust it with a little icing sugar. Place the parchment paper, sugar-side down, over the cake then carefully flip the baking sheet over. Remove the baking sheet and carefully peel off the parchment paper used for baking. Use a 20 cm (8 inch) pastry ring (or a plate and a knife) to cut the cake into two circles.

Line the sides of the 20 cm (8 inch) pastry ring or springform pan with a strip of acetate (best) or parchment paper.

→

To finish making the filling, in a large bowl, combine the drained ricotta and vanilla.

In the bowl of a stand mixer fitted with the whisk attachment, whip the double whipping cream and icing sugar until stiff peaks form, being careful to not overwhip the cream. Add the whipped cream to the ricotta mixture and use a rubber spatula to fold it in by hand. Transfer the ricotta mousse filling to a piping bag.

Place one cake layer inside the prepared pastry ring or springform pan. This is the base of the cake.

Use scissors to cut the tip of the ricotta mousse–filled piping bag and pipe the ricotta mousse on top of the cake and halfway up the sides of the pastry ring or springform pan. Sprinkle most of the mini chocolate chips and the strawberries on the ricotta mousse filling then pipe more of the ricotta mousse filling on top. Use an off-set spatula to spread the filling into a smooth, even layer. Place the second cake layer on top, pressing it gently into the filling, then place the cake in the freezer for at least 2 hours. (At this point, the cake can be wrapped in plastic wrap and frozen for up to 2 months; once it's defrosted, the cake should be enjoyed within 1 day.)

About 30 minutes before serving, take the cake out of the freezer and remove the pastry ring or release and remove the sides of the springform pan. Peel off the acetate or parchment paper and generously dust the cake with icing sugar. Decorate the top of the cake with strawberries and enjoy.

Torta Mazzini

INGREDIENTS

Makes 1 cake
(21.5 cm / 8 ½ inch)
Makes about 10 servings

- 120 g (¾ cup plus 1½ tablespoons) blanched whole almonds
- 120 g (½ cup plus 4 teaspoons) granulated sugar, plus more for sprinkling
- 2 large organic egg yolks, at room temperature, plus 2 large organic egg whites, at room temperature
- Zest and juice of 1 organic lemon
- 1½ teaspoons pure vanilla extract or paste (or the seeds of 1½ vanilla bean pods)
- Pinch of fine salt
- 1 sheet all-butter puff pastry
- Icing sugar (confectioners' sugar), for dusting

NOTE For this recipe, I recommend using high-quality purchased puff pastry to keep it easy, but if you want to prepare your own, you can find the recipe on page 26.

Giuseppe Mazzini, born in Genova (Genoa) in 1805, was a nationalist and a patriot. Along with Giuseppe Garibaldi, Camillo Benso, Count of Cavour, and Victor Emmanuel II, Mazzini was a crucial part of the Italian Risorgimento. A man with a strong vision for Italy, he was also known to be a real dessert lover! According to legend, when Mazzini was exiled in Switzerland, he used to write to his mother, Maria Drago, who still lived in Genova. One day, he asked if she could bake a cake he had tasted in Grenchen and shared a recipe that looked incomplete and quite generic. Mazzini's mother baked the cake, which became what we know today as "Torta Mazzini". Or so the story says...and I love stories like this!

METHOD Preheat the oven to 170°C (335°F). Grease a 21.5 cm (8½ inch) springform pan then line the bottom with parchment paper.

In a food processor or blender, combine the almonds and 2 tablespoons of the granulated sugar and blend until finely ground.

In the bowl of a stand mixer fitted with the whisk attachment, whip the remaining sugar and the egg yolks until creamy and glossy. Add the lemon zest and juice and the vanilla, followed by the finely ground almond mixture. Transfer this mixture to a large bowl.

Clean and thoroughly dry the stand mixer bowl and the whisk attachment. Add the egg whites and salt whip on high until stiff. Add the whipped egg whites to the egg yolk mixture and use a rubber spatula to gently fold them together, being careful to not deflate the batter.

Cut the puff pastry into a circle to fit the prepared pan then arrange it inside. Use a fork to prick the puff pastry all over to prevent air pockets from forming in the oven. Pour the egg and almond mixture on top of the puff pastry then dust with some icing sugar and sprinkle with some granulated sugar. Bake for 35 to 40 minutes, or until golden. Place the pan on a rack, release and remove the sides of the pan, and let the cake cool completely. The cake can be stored in an airtight container at room temperature for up to 2 days.

Melissa's

FUTURE

"You can't go back and make
a new start, but you can start
right now and make
a brand-new ending."

J. SHERMAN

Dear future,

I don't know you; no one does and yet we are all so very scared of you. Maybe, if we all knew you, you wouldn't be so scary anymore, but where's the fun in that? For many years, I have tried to control you, tailor you, and make you the way I imagined you to be, but the more I tried, the more I failed. I had to come to terms with the fact that I have no power over you. Of course, I make choices every day, and through those choices, I hope to shape you the best way for myself, but who knows if I am doing it right? Some of us, the wiser ones, understand that fighting you is a losing battle, and they don't want to be frightened anymore. And besides, why should we fear what has yet to hurt us?!?

It must look as though we are all running around like crazy horses, trying to catch you and win over you—as if we could! We are taught that we need to be mentally and economically ready for when you come to get us, but in the end, no matter how prepared we all are, you come to fetch us and eventually, we all go to the same place, which no one can really prepare for. How ironic! It seems to me like a real waste of time.

I am learning to stay put and to enjoy whatever comes. Even troubles have a purpose, and if I look at them from another perspective, I see them as precious gifts.

You know, it's not all that bad down here. There are so many beautiful things still left ...

I see many people changing for the best, learning the true value of things, and working for a better you—a better future. Others are still yet to understand, but I am hopeful.

If I had to imagine you, dear future, I picture you as the colour white, as a blank canvas, on which we can draw, using all the colours in the world! It would be so nice...

If you were a dessert or a cake (You know I bake cakes, right? Actually, you helped me become a baker, and I can't thank you enough for that!), I imagine you to be protective of traditions but also open to a new way of baking. I see you embracing a more inclusive way in which every-one, regardless of their dietary choices or health, can enjoy a moment of delight. Food has this amazing power to bring people together, and I wish for you to help us connect to one another, without prejudice. It's incredible, I know, but believe me, dear future, cakes and food in general have this power! They are a very strong weapon, but not everyone understands this yet. Could you do something about this? Can you help? If you think about it, people making more ethical choices will shape you in a better way and will make your work easier! I hope we can all work together on this. In my small way, I make my contribution and believe me, it's not that hard. Doing just a little is enough to make the difference...but you already know this.

Personally, I don't need to ask you for much. Well, none of the things I have imagined have gone as planned, but nonetheless, you have been very kind to me, and I thank you for this. I made plenty of mistakes, but I want to believe I did good, too. Anyway, I can't change the past, but I can work with you. You made me who I am, through some tough lessons, but all in all, I cannot complain. I simply want to be able to do better, for myself and for those I love. May I ask for a favour, dear future? Please allow me to be a baker for as long as I will live. It's truly what makes me happy and warms my heart, and I don't want to lose that. I have been fully committed since I started, and I have gone where I never thought I could!

I know my words are simple, but I am on a quest to make everything simple. To have a simple life; to bake simply because I enjoy it; to simply share what I have and what I have learned with people; to simply move forward, respecting every living creature; and to be simply true to myself. It's that simple!

Ok, I have nothing else to add. I am here, waiting for you. It will be wonderful to meet you and I hope you will be kind to me and to all. I know you can be, but I also know that we need to play our part, too.

See you soon!
Yours sincerely,

MELISSA

P.S I'm not scared
of you anymore.

Torta al limone e mirtilli

LEMON AND BLUEBERRY CAKE

INGREDIENTS

Makes 1 (20 cm / 8 inch) cake
Makes about 8 servings

- 330 g (2¼ cups plus 2 tablespoons) plain flour (all-purpose flour)
- 260 g (1¼ cups plus 2 teaspoons) granulated sugar
- 1 tablespoon baking powder
- Pinch of fine salt
- 200 ml (¾ cup plus 4 teaspoons) almond milk or other plant-based milk
- 130 ml (½ cup plus 2 teaspoons) vegetable oil, preferably non-GMO
- Zest and juice of 3 organic lemons
- 2 teaspoons pure vanilla extract or paste (or the seeds of 2 vanilla bean pods)
- 250 g (8¾ ounces) fresh blueberries, plus more for decorating
- Icing sugar (confectioners' sugar), for decorating

NOTE You can use frozen blueberries or any kind of berry you like—there's no need to thaw them before using.

I cannot stress this enough: I love simple cakes, the kind of cakes that have a rustic look and are all about the flavour! This cake has tons of flavour, and you definitely don't have to be vegan to enjoy it! It's one of those simple, beautiful, and delicious cakes that is perfect for leaving in the kitchen, on a pretty cake stand, so the entire family can have a piece at any time! This cake is also super easy to make. You don't need a stand mixer, just a bowl and a whisk. YEAH!!!

METHOD Preheat the oven to 180°C (350°F). Grease a 20 cm (8 inch) springform pan then line the bottom with parchment paper.

Place 1 tablespoon of the plain flour in a medium bowl and set aside.

Sift the remaining plain flour into a large bowl. Add the granulated sugar, baking powder, and salt. Whisk to combine and remove any lumps.

In a medium jug or bowl, whisk together the almond milk, vegetable oil, lemon zest and juice, and the vanilla. While whisking constantly, gradually pour this mixture into the flour mixture and continue whisking just until combined, being careful not to overmix the batter!

Add the blueberries to the bowl with the 1 tablespoon of plain flour and toss to coat—this prevents the berries from sinking to the bottom of the batter. Gently fold the flour-coated blueberries into the batter. Pour the batter into the prepared pan and bake for 40 to 45 minutes, or until a wooden pick inserted in the centre comes out almost clean. I like this cake to be moist and slightly underbaked. Place the pan on a rack and let the cake cool for about 10 minutes then release and remove the sides of the pan and let the cake cool completely. When the completely cool, decorate it with more blueberries, dust with icing sugar, and..... Voilà! This cake can be stored in an airtight container at room temperature for up to 3 days.

L'unica torta al cioccolato vegana di cui hai bisogno

THE ONLY VEGAN CHOCOLATE CAKE YOU NEED

INGREDIENTS
Makes 1 (23 cm / 9 inch) cake
Makes about 10 to 12 servings

For the cake

· 250 g (1¾ cup plus ½ tablespoon) plain flour (all-purpose flour)
· 160 g (¾ cup plus 1 tablespoon) granulated sugar
· 160 g (¾ cup plus 2 teaspoons) light brown sugar
· 1½ teaspoons baking powder
· 1½ teaspoons baking soda
· Pinch of fine salt
· 250 ml (1 cup plus 2 teaspoons) soy milk
· 1 tablespoon white vinegar
· 220 g (7¾ ounces) vegan dark chocolate, chopped
· 240 ml (1 cup) boiling water
· 55 g (½ cup plus 3 tablespoons) unsweetened cocoa powder
· 180 g (¾ cup) applesauce
· 50 ml (3½ tablespoons) fresh brewed espresso coffee, still warm
· 1 tablespoon pure vanilla extract or paste (or the seeds of 3 vanilla bean pods)
· 130 ml (½ cup plus 2 teaspoons) vegetable oil, preferably non-GMO

For the frosting

· 350 g (12¼ ounces) vegan dark chocolate, chopped
· 35 g (7 tablespoons) unsweetened cocoa powder
· 400 g (14 ounces coconut cream (not coconut milk)
· 1½ teaspoons pure vanilla extract or paste (or the seeds of 1½ vanilla bean pods)

The title of this recipe says it all: This is an absolutely essential cake to have in your vegan recipe repertoire. With this cake as your base, you can create hundreds of different flavour combinations, adding fruit, nuts, a vegan caramel sauce, or more chocolate—maybe even white chocolate. Or you can simply leave it as is, plain and simple. Birthdays, Valentine's Day, and other celebrations are not going to be a problem anymore!

METHOD For the cake, preheat the oven to 170°C (335°F). Grease two 23 cm (9 inch) round cake pans then line the bottoms with parchment paper.

In a large bowl, whisk together the plain flour, granulated sugar, brown sugar, baking powder, baking soda, and salt.

In a large bowl, combine the soy milk and white vinegar and let stand for 10 minutes to create vegan buttermilk.

Place the dark chocolate in a medium bowl then pour the boiling water over it. Let stand for few minutes then stir to melt the chocolate. Add the cocoa powder and stir to combine.

Add the applesauce, espresso, and vanilla to the vegan buttermilk. Add the chocolate mixture and vegetable oil and stir to combine. Add the flour mixture and whisk to combine. Divide the batter between the prepared pans and bake for about 40 minutes, or until a wooden pick inserted in the centre of each cake comes out clean. Place the pans on a rack and let the cakes cool for about

20 minutes then invert the cakes onto the rack and let them cool completely at room temperature.

For the frosting, place the dark chocolate and cocoa powder in a medium bowl.

In a medium saucepan, warm the coconut cream over medium heat until hot enough to melt the chocolate; don't let it come to a boil. Pour it over the dark chocolate and cocoa powder, add the vanilla, and stir until smooth. Refrigerate for at least 40 minutes, or until it's thick enough to frost the cake.

When the frosting is ready, place one cake layer on a cake board or serving plate. Use a rubber spatula to spread some frosting on top then place the second cake layer on top. Frost the top and sides of the cake. Use your creativity to decorate the cake and have fun!

NOTE To make your own applesauce, peel, core, and chop 2 apples. In a small saucepan, bring the apples and a little water to a boil then mash them with a fork; no sugar required. Be sure to use coconut cream, not coconut milk, to make the frosting—they are different ingredients.

Crostata frangipane alle albicocche

APRICOT FRANGIPANE TART

INGREDIENTS
Makes 1 (25 cm / 10 inch) tart
Makes about 10 to 12 servings

For the pastry dough

· 220 g (1½ cups plus 1 tablespoon) plain flour (all-purpose flour)
· 60 g (½ cup) almond flour
· 60 g (½ cup) icing sugar (confectioners' sugar), plus more for dusting
· Pinch of fine salt
· 160 g (½ cup plus 3 tablespoons) unsalted vegan butter, cold and cut into pieces

for the filling

· 220 g (1¾ cups plus 1 tablespoon) almond flour
· 70 g (½ cup) plain flour (all-purpose flour)
· 125 g (½ cup plus 2 tablespoons) granulated sugar
· 35g (3½ tablespoons) cornstarch, preferably organic
· 1 teaspoon baking powder
· 168 g (¾ cup) unsalted vegan butter, melted and cooled
· 120 ml (½ cup) almond milk
· 1 teaspoon pure almond extract
· 1 teaspoon pure vanilla extract or paste (or the seeds of 1 vanilla bean pod)
· About 3 tablespoons apricot jam, plus more for glazing (optional)
· About 20 canned apricot halves, drained
· 60 g (½ cup plus 1 tablespoon) sliced almond

NOTE You can make the pastry dough by hand, but using a food processor is quicker. Just make sure not to blend the ingredients too much or the heat of the food processor blade will melt the vegan butter.

I wanted to write about a classic dessert, which are often a problem for vegans to find in cafés. Apricots and frangipane are a match made in heaven, but I recommend trying other types of fruit, such as peaches or even pineapple! I love to offer alternatives, so you can take my recipes and make them your own—and even more special!

METHOD For the pastry dough, in the bowl of a food processor, combine the plain flour, almond flour, icing sugar, and salt. Add the butter and process until the mixture is sandy. Gradually add just enough chilled water to bring the ingredients together and form a dough—about 2 tablespoons. Gather the dough into a bowl without kneading it then wrap it in plastic wrap and refrigerate it for at least 1 hour and preferably overnight.

When the pastry dough has chilled, grease a 25 cm (10 inch) round fluted tart tin then line the bottom with parchment paper.

On a lightly floured work surface, use a rolling pin to roll out the dough into a circle large enough to fit into the bottom and up the sides of the tart tin. Lift the pastry dough and press it into the prepared tart tin. Trim any excess dough and use a fork to prick the entire base of the tart. Place the tart shell in the freezer for about 30 minutes.

Preheat the oven to 170°C (335°F). Line the tart shell with a piece of parchment paper then fill it with baking beans or rice. Blind bake the tart shell for about 20 minutes then remove the baking beans or rice and the parchment paper and bake the tart shell for about 10 more minutes, or until set but still pale. Place the tart tin on a rack and let the tart shell cool at room temperature. Leave the oven on.

→

→

For the filling, in a large bowl, whisk together the almond flour, plain flour, granulated sugar, cornstarch, and baking powder. Add the melted and cooled butter, almond milk, almond extract, and vanilla. Stir until smooth and creamy.

Use the back of a spoon to spread the apricot jam evenly in the bottom of the cooled tart shell then spread the frangipane evenly on top. Press the apricots halves, cut-side down, into the frangipane then sprinkle the sliced almonds on top. Bake for about 50 minutes, or until a wooden pick inserted in the centre comes out clean. Place the tart tin on a rack and let the tart cool completely before carefully removing the sides. Dust some icing sugar over the top, or even better, use a pastry brush to glaze the tart with some extra apricot jam. Cut into slices and serve. This tart can be stored in an airtight container in the refrigerator for up to 3 days.

Torta Bundt al limone

LEMON BUNDT CAKE

INGREDIENTS

**Makes 1 Bundt cake
(25 cm / 10 inch)**
Makes about 10 to 12 servings

For the cake

- 440 g (3 cups plus
  2 tablespoons) plain flour
  (all-purpose flour)
- 3 tablespoons cornstarch,
  preferably organic
- 2½ teaspoons baking
  powder
- Pinch of fine salt
- Zest and juice
  of 3 organic lemons
- 400 g (2 cups)
  granulated sugar
- 415 ml (1¾ cups) almond
  milk or other
  plant-based milk
- 145 ml (½ cup plus 4
  teaspoons) vegetable oil,
  preferably non-GMO
- 2 teaspoons pure vanilla
  extract or paste (or the
  seeds of 2 vanilla bean pods)
- 1 teaspoon pure lemon oil
  (optional, for extra
  lemon flavour)
- 90 g (6 tablespoons)
  applesauce

For decoration

- Icing sugar
  (confectioners' sugar)

NOTE To make your own applesauce, peel, core, and chop 1 apple. In a small saucepan, bring the apple and a little water to a boil then mash them with a fork; no sugar required.

In all my books, you can always find recipes using Bundt pans and you can always find recipes using lemons. The reason? I simply love Bundt cakes and I adore the flavour of fresh lemons! I'm often asked what my favourite cake is and, well, I think you can guess that it's lemon cake—lemon cake in any form! This vegan lemon Bundt cake is lovely! It's fresh, simple, and always a winner! You can experiment with different Bundt pans, but I recommend skipping the silicone ones and sticking to metal pans. While I like silicone moulds for frozen desserts, I'm not a fan of baking with them and find metal pans more reliable. Metal pans also last forever! I own, and still use, antique Bundt pans I found in antique markets, and they are still perfect in shape and bake beautifully!

METHOD For the cake, preheat the oven to 170°C (335°F). Generously grease a 25 cm (10 inch) Bundt pan.

In a large bowl, whisk together the plain flour, cornstarch, baking powder, and salt. Add the lemon zest.

In a medium jug or bowl, whisk together the granulated sugar, almond milk, vegetable oil, lemon juice, vanilla, and lemon oil, if using. Add the applesauce and mix to combine. Add this mixture to the flour mixture and whisk until smooth. Pour the batter into the prepared pan and bake for about 50 minutes, or until a wooden pick inserted in the centre comes out clean. Place the pan on a rack and let the cake cool for about 15 minutes then carefully invert the cake onto the rack and let it cool completely at room temperature.

To finish, dust with icing sugar. This cake can be stored in an airtight container at room temperature for up to 4 days.

Fette di zenzero

GINGER CAKE

INGREDIENTS
Makes about 8 servings

For the cake
- 440 g (3 cups plus 2 tablespoons) plain flour (all-purpose flour)
- 5 teaspoons ground ginger
- 1½ teaspoons ground cinnamon
- 1½ teaspoons baking powder
- 1 teaspoon baking soda
- ¼ teaspoon freshly grated nutmeg
- 2 cloves, crushed
- Zest of 1 organic orange
- 1½ teaspoons pure vanilla extract or paste (or the seeds of 1½ vanilla bean pods)
- 160 g (¾ cup plus 1 tablespoon) caster sugar (superfine sugar)
- ½ tsp salt
- 350 ml (1¼ cups plus 3½ tablespoons) boiling water
- 160 ml (⅔ cup) vegetable oil, preferably non-GMO
- 200 g (7 ounces) golden syrup
- 200 g (7 ounces) treacle

For the glaze
- 80 g (⅔ cup) icing sugar (confectioners' sugar)
- 2 to 3 teaspoons lemon juice

NOTE You can use maple syrup in place of the golden syrup, but the flavour will be different

Here is a super easy cake that makes a wonderful gift to bring to the office as a present before the holidays—you can also put slices in small bags and close them with festive ribbon. Serve this cake after Christmas dinner or for a spicy Christmas Day breakfast! Ginger = CHRISTMAS! There's no argument on that, right?

METHOD For the cake, preheat the oven to 170°C (335°F). Grease a 23 x 33 cm (9 x 13 inch) rectangular cake tin or deep baking sheet then line the bottom with parchment paper.

Sift the plain flour, ginger, cinnamon, baking powder, baking soda, and nutmeg into a large bowl. Add the crushed cloves, orange zest, vanilla, caster sugar, and salt and stir to incorporate.

In a medium jug or bowl, combine the boiling water, vegetable oil, golden syrup, and treacle and stir until fully combined. Add this mixture to the flour mixture and stir to fully combine. Pour the batter into the prepared pan and bake for about 30 minutes, or until a wooden pick inserted in the centre comes out clean. Place the cake tin on a rack and let the cake cool completely at room temperature then invert the cake onto a serving plate.

For the glaze, place the icing sugar in a small bowl. Whisk in enough lemon juice to achieve a thick yet pourable consistency. Drizzle the glaze all over the cake then cut the cake into squares and serve. This cake can be stored in an airtight container at room temperature for up to 3 days.

Bignè alla crema chantilly

CHANTILLY CREAM BIGNÈ

INGREDIENTS
Makes about 12 servings

For the chantilly cream
- 130 ml (½ cup plus 2 teaspoons) oat milk
- 30 g (¼ cup) icing sugar (confectioners' sugar), plus more for dusting
- 1 teaspoon pure vanilla extract or paste (or the seeds of 1 vanilla bean pod)
- 120 g (½ cup plus 1 teaspoon) unsalted vegan butter, cut into small pieces
- 250 ml (1 cup plus 2 teaspoons) vegan double whipping cream, chilled

For the choux pastry
- 4 teaspoons granulated sugar
- 35 g (3½ tablespoons) cornstarch, preferably organic
- ½ teaspoon baking powder
- 250 g (8¾ ounces) soy milk
- 50 g (3½ tablespoons) cocoa butter
- 15 g (1/2 ounce) rice oil
- Pinch of fine salt
- 110 g (¾ cup plus ½ tablespoon) plain flour (all-purpose flour)
- 130 g (4 ½ ounces) room temperature water

For the glaze
- 80 g (⅔ cup) icing sugar (confectioners' sugar)
- 2 to 3 teaspoons lemon juice

NOTE I don't use margarine, but you can use it in place of the vegan butter in the chantilly cream. If you want to use the choux pastry to make éclairs, use a small or medium star pastry tip.

One of most difficult aspects of vegan and gluten-free baking is using the right alternative ingredients to maintain a soft texture or achieve the correct rise. I try to keep my recipes as simple as possible and rarely add alternative ingredients unless it's really necessary. For this recipe, I had to use cocoa butter and rice oil, but they are both very easy to source in shops—even average supermarkets. With this recipe, you will be able to make Bignè and éclairs. You can even use the dough as a base to make savoury cream puffs! Fun! Fun! Fun!

METHOD For the chantilly cream, in a medium saucepan, combine the oat milk, icing sugar, and vanilla and bring to a boil over medium heat. Add the butter and use an immersion blender to blend until smooth. Transfer the mixture to a large bowl, cover with plastic wrap, and refrigerate overnight; it needs to chill for that long to reach the right consistency.

For the choux pastry, preheat the oven to 190°C (375°F). Line one or two baking sheets with parchment paper. Fit a piping bag with a small or medium round pastry tip. Fit a second piping bag with a small or medium star pastry tip.

In a medium bowl, whisk together the granulated sugar, cornstarch, and baking powder.

In a medium saucepan, bring the soy milk, cocoa butter, rice oil, and salt to a gentle boil over medium heat. Remove the pan from the heat then add the plain flour, along with the granulated sugar mixture, and use a wooden spoon and a lot of elbow grease to vigorously beat together. Add the water and continue beating until a dough is formed. Transfer the dough to the piping bag fitted with the round pastry tip and pipe Bignè onto the prepared baking sheets, leaving room for expansion. Bake for about 14 minutes then open the oven door slightly (leave the oven on) and continue baking for 5 to 8 more minutes. Place the baking sheets on a rack and let the Bignè cool completely at room temperature.

To finish making the chantilly cream, in the bowl of a stand mixer fitted with the whisk attachment, whip the double whipping cream until stiff peaks form. Add the chilled oat milk mixture and gently fold to combine. Transfer the chantilly cream to the piping bag fitted with the star tip. Use the pastry tip to poke a hole in the bottom of each Bignè then squeeze chantilly cream inside until the Bignè feel heavy. Alternatively, cut the Bignè in half, pipe a rosette right in the centre of each bottom half and top with the Bignè tops. For the glaze, place the icing sugar in a small bowl. Whisk in enough lemon juice to achieve a thick yet pourable consistency. Cover the top of the Bignè with the glaze. Bignè are best enjoyed the day they are made.

Torta quadrata ai mirtilli

BLUEBERRY BARS

INGREDIENTS

Makes about 8 bars

For the crust and crumble

· 2 tablespoons coconut oil,
  preferably organic,
  or vegetable oil, preferably
  non-GMO
· 215 g (7 ½ ounces)
  maple syrup
· 1 tablespoon oat milk,
  plus more as needed
· 160 g (1¼ cups) almond flour
· 160 g (1 cup plus 2
  tablespoons) plain flour
  (all-purpose flour)
· Pinch of fine salt

For the blueberry compote

· 500 g (17½ ounces)
  blueberries
· 190 g (6¾ ounces)
  maple syrup
· Zest of 1 organic lemon
· 2½ tablespoons cornstarch,
  preferably organic

NOTE You can use honey in
place of the maple syrup,
but the bars will be sweeter.

A blueberry tart is one of those well-known and well-loved desserts that one MUST make at least once. But these vegan bars are a great alternative. Cut into squares, they make a great snack for the office, or a lovely afternoon treat for your kids. They're also packed with vitamins. Easy, quick, and healthy—what else can we hope for?

METHOD For the crust and crumble, preheat the oven to 170°C (335°F). Line a 23 cm (9 inch) square cake pan with parchment paper, leaving extra paper hanging over the sides to make it easier to remove the bars after baking.

Place a little water in a saucepan set over medium heat and bring to a boil. Place the coconut oil in a large bowl then place the bowl over the saucepan, making sure the bowl doesn't touch the water. Melt the coconut oil completely then remove the bowl from the saucepan and add the maple syrup, oat milk, almond flour, plain flour, and salt. Mix with your hands until a dough is formed. If the dough is too dry, add a dash more oat milk. Divide the dough in half. Wrap one portion in plastic wrap and place it in the fridge. Press the remaining portion into the prepared pan, using your fingers to push the dough all the way to the edges. Bake for 10 to 12 minutes, or until the crumble looks nicely golden. Place the pan on a rack and let the crust cool. Leave the oven on.

For the blueberry compote, combine the blueberries, maple syrup, and lemon zest in a medium saucepan with a lid. Cover and cook over low heat until the blueberries are soft.

In a small glass, combine the cornstarch with a little water and whisk until the cornstarch is completely dissolved. Add this mixture to the blueberries and cook for about 3 minutes, or until thick. Pour the blueberry compote into the prebaked crust, spreading it evenly with a spatula. Take the remaining portion of dough out of the fridge and use your fingers to crumble it all over the compote, covering it completely. Bake for 20 to 25 minutes, or until the crumble is golden. Cool the bars completely before cutting them into squares and serving. This cake can be stored in an airtight container at room temperature for up to 3 days.

Vegan scones

INGREDIENTS
Makes 12 scones

- 250 g (8 ¾ ounces) soy milk
- 1 tablespoon white vinegar
- 380 g (3¼ cups) 00 flour
- 3 tablespoons
  granulated sugar
- 1 tablespoon baking powder
- 1 teaspoon baking soda
- Pinch of fine salt
- 100 g (7 tablespoons)
  vegan butter, cold
  and cut into small pieces

NOTE The secret to soft scones is to mix and touch the batter as little as possible. You can make smaller scones, but you'll need to adjust the baking time.

I must admit, that for this recipe, I cheated a little! I basically took my recipe for the scones we serve at Café Duse and swapped normal buttermilk for vegan buttermilk and normal butter for vegan butter. I did it because it's possible, and the results are just as delicious. See, vegan baking can be easy! The only thing left to do now is put the kettle on and serve tea!

METHOD Preheat the oven to 200°C (400°F). Line a baking sheet with parchment paper.

In a large bowl, combine the soy milk and white vinegar and let stand for 10 minutes to create vegan buttermilk.

In the bowl of a food processor, combine the 00 flour, granulated sugar, baking powder, baking soda, and salt. Briefly stir with a spoon to combine. Add the butter and pulse until the mixture is sandy, being careful to not overprocess the dough. Transfer the mixture to a large bowl, add the buttermilk, and gently but quickly mix until a rough dough forms. Drop the dough onto a lightly floured work surface and gather it into a rough ball. It will look grainy, lumpy, and messy, but don't worry; it's meant to look like that. Using your hands, roughly flatten the dough until it's about 2.5 cm (1 inch) thick. Using a 5 cm (2 inch) round pastry cutter, cut the dough into rounds and place them on the prepared baking sheet. Bake for about 10 minutes, or until lightly golden. Serve warm. These scones are best enjoyed the day they are baked.

Flan vegano

VEGAN FLAN

INGREDIENTS

Makes 1 (20 cm / 8 inch) flan
Makes about 8 servings

For the pastry dough

· 210 g (1½ cups) plain flour
  (all-purpose flour)
· 2 tablespoons
  granulated sugar
· 110 g (7 tablespoons plus
  2 teaspoons) unsalted vegan
  butter, cut into small pieces
· ½ tablespoon ice water

for the filling

· 180 g (¾ cup plus
  2 tablespoons)
  granulated sugar
· 50 g (5 tablespoons)
  cornstarch, preferably
  organic
· 35 g (2 full tablespoons)
  vanilla pudding mix powder
· 1½ teaspoons agar-agar
  powder
· 1 teaspoon ground turmeric
· ¼ teaspoon fine salt
· 1 L (4½ cups) organic
  almond milk or soy milk
· 110 g (7 tablespoons plus
  2 teaspoons) unsalted
  vegan butter
· 2½ teaspoons pure vanilla
  extract or paste (or the
  seeds of 2½ vanilla bean
  pods)

NOTE Vanilla pudding mix
powder happens to be natural-
ly vegan. Be sure to use blocks
of vegan butter rather than the
spreadable variety. I recommend using a food processor,
but you can make this dough
by hand; it will just take longer.

I think of flan as fancy and rather la-
bour-intensive to make, but this
vegan flan is not that intimidating.
I reckon it can be a very elegant dessert for a lovely dinner party and can
be made year-round. The decoration
should be simple and classic. In fact,
sometimes, I don't decorate the flan at
all! I think it looks pretty just as it is...

METHOD For the pastry dough, preheat
the oven to 180°C (350°F). Grease a 20
cm (8 inch) springform pan then line the
bottom with parchment paper.

In the bowl of a food processor, combine
the plain flour, granulated sugar, vegan
butter, and ice water and pulse until a
dough forms. Wrap the dough in plastic
wrap and refrigerate for at least 30 minutes to set.

When the dough has chilled, on a lightly
floured work surface, use a rolling pin
to roll out the dough until about 3 mm
(⅛ inch). Carefully lift the pastry dough
and push it into the prepared pan, covering the entire base and going about
5 cm (2 inches) up the sides. Trim any
excess dough then place the pan in the
freezer while you make the filling.

For the filling, in a medium saucepan,
whisk together the granulated sugar,
cornstarch, vanilla pudding mix, agar-
agar powder, turmeric, and salt. Add
about 90 ml (6 tablespoons) of the almond milk and stir until the sugar mixture is completely dissolved. Add the remaining almond milk and place the pan

→

→

over medium heat. Add the vegan butter and cook, stirring constantly, until simmering. Once the mixture is simmering, remove from the heat, add the vanilla, and quickly stir to combine. It's important to work quickly because the agar-agar will quickly set the mixture.

Take the pastry dough base out of the freezer and pour the filling on top. Bake for 35 to 40 minutes. Remove the flan from the oven, place a sheet of aluminium foil on top, and bake for 10 to 15 more minutes, or until the flan is set but still jiggles slightly. Place the pan on a rack and let the flan cool at room temperature. Refrigerate the flan overnight and serve the next day.

Biscotti di Natale

CHRISTMAS COOKIES

INGREDIENTS
Makes about 12 cookies

- 140 g (1 cup plus 3 tablespoons) gluten-free 00 flour
- 50 g (6 tablespoons) almond flour
- 100 g (½ cup) brown sugar
- Zest of 1 organic orange (optional)
- 1 teaspoon baking powder
- ½ teaspoon ground ginger
- ½ teaspoon ground cinnamon
- ¼ teaspoon ground cardamom
- 1 clove, crushed
- Pinch of fine salt
- 113 g (½ cup) unsalted vegan butter, at room temperature
- 60 g (¼ cup) molasses
- 1½ teaspoons pure vanilla extract or paste (or the seeds of 1½ vanilla bean pods)
- Granulated sugar, for decorating

NOTE The orange zest is optional but highly recommended.

There are countless recipes for Christmas cookies, I am well aware, but I still wish to share mine with you. There's no need for fancy ingredients or tools. These cookies simply taste and smell like the holidays!

METHOD In a large bowl, whisk together the 00 flour, almond flour, brown sugar, orange zest, if using, baking powder, ginger, cinnamon, cardamom, clove, and salt.

In the bowl of a stand mixer fitted with the paddle attachment, beat the butter and molasses until combined then add the vanilla. With the mixer on low, add the flour mixture and beat until a dough forms. On a lightly floured work surface, gather the dough into a ball, wrap it in plastic wrap, and refrigerate it for at least 1 hour.

When the dough has chilled, preheat the oven to 170°C (335°F). Line a baking sheet with parchment paper. Put some granulated sugar in a medium bowl.

Divide the dough into twelve equal pieces. Roll each piece into a ball then roll the balls in the granulated sugar and arrange on the prepared baking sheet. Using the palm of your hand, flatten each ball into the baking sheet. Bake for about 10 minutes. Place the baking sheet on a rack and let the biscotti cool before serving. These cookies can be stored in an airtight container at room temperature for about 5 days

Torta al cioccolato e nocciole

CHOCOLATE HAZELNUT CAKE

INGREDIENTS
Makes 1 (20 cm / 8 inch) cake
Makes about 10 servings

For the cake
· 130 g (1⅓ cups)
  gluten-free oats
· 70 g (½ cup plus
  1 tablespoons)
  whole hazelnuts
· 1 tablespoon unsweetened
  cocoa powder
· 55 g (2 ounces) coconut oil
· 2 tablespoons maple syrup

For the filling
· 600 ml (2½ cups)
  full-fat coconut milk
· 90 g (3¼ ounces)
  maple syrup
· 2 tablespoons coconut oil
· 1½ teaspoons pure vanilla
  extract or paste (or the
  seeds of 1½ vanilla
  bean pods)
· 480 g (16¾ ounces) vegan
  dark chocolate, at least 65%
  cacao, roughly chopped

What can I say about this recipe? It's a classic and I think this cake should be eaten and not explained. Plus, it's beautiful to look at! Don't you agree?

METHOD For the cake, preheat the oven to 170°C (335°F). Brush a 20 cm (8 inch) springform pan with coconut oil or vegetable oil.

In the bowl of a food processor, combine the oats, hazelnuts, and cocoa powder and pulse until combined. Add the coconut oil and maple syrup and pulse until fully combined. Use your hands to gather the dough (it will be moist) and gently press it into the bottom of the prepared pan. Bake for about 10 minutes, or until golden. Place the pan on a rack and let the cake cool while you make the filling.

For the filling, in a medium saucepan, combine the coconut milk, maple syrup, coconut oil, and vanilla over medium heat. When the mixture is warm, add the chocolate and stir until it's completely melted. Remove from the heat and let the mixture cool for about 8 minutes. Pour the chocolate mixture into the springform pan and refrigerate it for at least 3 hours to set. Remove the cake from the fridge 20 minutes before serving, release and remove the sides of the pan, and decorate the cake using your creativity.

Torta a strati al limone

LEMON LAYER CAKE

INGREDIENTS

Makes 1 (20 cm / 8 inch) cake
Makes about 12 servings

For the lemon curd

- Zest and juice
  of 4 organic lemons
- 226 g (1 cup) unsalted butter
- 280 g (1¼ cups plus
  2 tablespoons)
  granulated sugar
- 4 large organic eggs
- 1 tablespoon cornstarch,
  preferably organic

For the cake

- 200 g (1¼ cups plus
  3 tablespoons) gluten-free
  plain flour (all-purpose flour)
- 200 g (1⅔ cups) almond flour
- 2 teaspoons baking powder
- ¼ teaspoon fine salt
- 300 g (1½ cups)
  granulated sugar
- Zest of 3 organic lemons
- 250 g (1 cup plus 5 teaspoons)
  unsalted butter, at room
  temperature
- 2 teaspoons pure vanilla
  extract or paste (or the seeds
  of 2 vanilla bean pods)
- 5 large organic eggs

For the frosting

- 250 g (1 cup plus 2 teaspoons)
  mascarpone cheese
- 250 (2 cups plus 1 tablespoon)
  gluten-free icing sugar
  (confectioners' sugar)
- 500 ml (2 cups plus
  1 tablespoon) double
  whipping cream (heavy cream)

For decorating

- Fresh or candied lemons

NOTE Be sure to make the lemon
curd one day ahead.

If you are in search of a stunning cake
that tastes like summer, look no further. You can use this recipe as a base
for many variations. You can also add
white chocolate, fresh fruit, or both. Either way, it will be a success!

METHOD For the lemon curd, in a medium
saucepan, combine the lemon zest and
juice, butter, and granulated sugar and
bring to a gentle boil over medium heat.

In a medium bowl, whisk the eggs. Temper the eggs by adding a little bit of the
hot lemon mixture and quickly whisking—it's important to whisk quickly or
you will cook the eggs. Pour the tempered egg mixture into the saucepan,
place over medium heat, and whisk until
fully combined. Add the cornstarch and
whisk until the mixture starts to thicken. Remove from the heat and pour the
curd through a fine-mesh sieve set over
bowl. Cover the curd with plastic wrap,
pressing the plastic onto the surface of
the curd to prevent a skin from forming,
and let cool to room temperature. Refrigerate overnight to set the curd.

For the cake, preheat the oven to 170°C
(335°F). Grease two 20 cm (8 inch)
round cake pans then line the bottoms
with parchment paper.

In a medium bowl, whisk together the
plain flour, almond flour, baking powder, and salt.

In the bowl of a stand mixer fitted with
the paddle attachment, combine the
granulated sugar and lemon zest and
beat until the sugar is fully coated in
zest. Add the butter and vanilla and beat
until light and fluffy. Add the eggs, one
at a time, and beat until fully incorporated. With the mixer on low, add the

→

→

flour mixture in three additions and beat until just incorporated. Divide the batter between the prepared pans and bake for 35 to 40 minutes, or until a wooden pick inserted in the centre of each cake comes out clean. Place the pans on a rack and let the cakes cool for 10 minutes then invert the cakes onto the rack and let cool completely at room temperature.

Remove the curd from the fridge and divide it in half. One portion will be your filling, and one part will be incorporated into the frosting.

For the frosting, in a large bowl, use a rubber spatula to combine the mascarpone cheese, icing sugar, and one portion of the lemon curd until smooth and creamy.

In the bowl of a stand mixer fitted with the whisk attachment, whip the double whipping cream until stiff peaks form, being very careful not to curdle the cream. Add the mascarpone mixture and use a rubber spatula to fold it into the whipped cream.

Place one cake layer on a cake board, stand, or serving place. Use a rubber spatula to spread a layer of lemon curd evenly on top. Place the second cake layer on top then use an off-set spatula or cake scraper to frost the top and the sides of the cake with the lemon curd whipped cream frosting. Decorate with fresh or candied lemons and serve. This cake can be stored in an airtight container in the refrigerator for up to 3 days.

Galette alle albicocche

APRICOT GALETTE

INGREDIENTS
Makes about 6 to 8 servings

For the pastry dough
- 270 g (1¾ cup plus 2 tablespoons) gluten-free plain flour (all-purpose flour)
- 2 tablespoons granulated sugar
- 85 g (6 tablespoons) unsalted vegan butter, cold and cut into small pieces
- About 100 ml (6 tablespoons plus 2 teaspoons) ice water

For the filling
- 20 small fresh apricots, halved and pitted
- 80 g (2 ¾ ounces) maple syrup
- 2 teaspoons pure vanilla extract or paste (or the seeds of 2 vanilla bean pods)
- 2 teaspoons granulated sugar
- 1 tablespoon plant-based milk
- 1 tablespoon light brown sugar

This is a French classic—not an Italian recipe—but I had to add it to the list, because it is one of my personal favourites. Serving a galette will always make you the "Queen or King" of baking! Use whatever fruit you like, following the same exact method.

METHOD For the pastry dough, in the bowl of a food processor, pulse together the plain flour and granulated sugar. Add the butter and pulse until the mixture is sandy. Gradually add the ice water, little by little, adding more or less depending on the humidity in your kitchen. The dough should be smooth and not sticky. Gather the dough into a ball, wrap it in plastic wrap, and refrigerate for 1 hour.

For the filling, cut 10 apricots (20 halves) into pieces and place in a large saucepan. Add the maple syrup, cover, and bring to a boil over medium heat. Lower the heat, stir, and cook for about 5 minutes, or until the fruit is soft. Add the vanilla and cook, uncovered, for about 10 more minutes, or until the mixture is thick. Remove from the heat and let cool at room temperature.

When the apricot mixture is cool, use an immersion blender, to purée it into a jam, being careful to not process it too much. The filling can have bits and chunks here and there.

Cut the remaining apricots into wedges. Place them in a bowl, add the granulated sugar, and toss to coat.

Preheat the oven to 190°C (375°F). Line a baking sheet with parchment paper.

On a lightly floured work surface, use a rolling pin to roll out the pastry dough into a circle, about 30.5 cm (12 inch) in diameter. Carefully transfer the dough to the prepared baking sheet. Use a rubber spatula to spread the apricot compote evenly across the round of dough, leaving a roughly 2.5 cm (1 inch) border around the edges. Arrange the sugar tossed apricot wedges on top. Fold the edges of the dough up and over the apricots and brush the border with the plant-based milk. Sprinkle the dough with the brown sugar then bake the galette for about 40 minutes, or until golden. This galette is best enjoyed the day it is baked.

Biscotti alle mandorle

ALMOND BISCOTTI

INGREDIENTS
Makes about 12 biscotti

- 200 g (1⅔ cups) almond flour
- 1½ teaspoons cornstarch, preferably organic
- 1 teaspoon baking powder
- ¼ teaspoon fine salt
- 1 large organic egg, at room temperature
- 2 tablespoons plus 2 teaspoons light brown sugar
- 3 tablespoons unsalted butter (or vegan butter, for vegan biscotti), melted
- 1½ teaspoons pure vanilla extract or paste (or the seeds of 1½ vanilla bean pods)
- 1 teaspoon pure almond extract
- Zest of 1 organic orange

These cookies look like the popular "Cantucci", but they are slightly softer. They can be put in bags or jars to create a lovely Christmas gift, because they can be baked in advance and keep well stored in an airtight container.

METHOD Preheat the oven to 170°C (335°F). Line a baking sheet with parchment paper.

In a large bowl, whisk together the almond flour, cornstarch, baking powder, and salt.

In a large bowl, combine the egg, brown sugar, butter, vanilla, almond extract, and orange zest and stir with a spatula to fully combine. Add this mixture to the almond flour mixture and use your hands to knead until a dough forms. Shape the dough into a log, measuring about 25 cm (10 inches) in length and about 6 cm (2½ inches) in width. Place it on the prepared baking sheet and bake for about 20 minutes, or until slightly golden. Remove the log from the oven and turn the oven temperature to 135°C (275°F). Use a serrated knife to carefully cut the dough log diagonally into slices, each about 2 cm (¾ inch thick). Place the slices back on the baking sheet and bake for 20 more minutes, or until the biscotti are golden. If the biscotti are turning too golden, flip them over, so they cook on the other side. Turn the oven off and let the biscotti cool with the oven door cracked open—you can use a wooden spoon to prop it open. Place the baking sheet on a rack and let the biscotti cool before serving. The biscotti can be stored in an airtight container at room temperature for up to 5 days.

Loaf 4/4

4/4 (POUND CAKE)

INGREDIENTS

Makes 1 loaf cake
(23 x 13 cm / 9 x 5 inch)
Makes about 10 servings

For the cake

- 280 g (2 cups) gluten-free plain flour (all-purpose flour)
- 1 teaspoon baking powder
- ½ teaspoon baking soda
- Pinch of fine salt
- 140 g (½ cup plus 4 teaspoons) unsalted butter, at room temperature
- 120 g (½ cup) gluten-free spreadable cream cheese, at room temperature
- 300 g (1½ cups) granulated sugar
- 2 teaspoons pure vanilla extract or paste (or the seeds of 2 vanilla bean pods)
- Zest and juice of 2 organic lemons
- 4 large organic eggs, at room temperature
- 70 ml (¼ cup plus 2 teaspoons) whole milk

For the glaze

- 250 g (2 cups plus 1 tablespoon) icing sugar (confectioners' sugar)
- Juice of about 2 organic lemons

Every baker should have a pound cake recipe in their recipe book. Pound cakes are undeniably good and so versatile, as they can be used as a base for many variations. Of course, I felt it was necessary to share a gluten-free version, so everyone can enjoy a delicious 4/4 cake!

METHOD For the cake, preheat the oven to 170°C (335°F). Grease a 23 x 13 cm (9 x 5 inch) loaf pan and line it with parchment paper.

Sift the plain flour, baking powder, baking soda, and salt into a large bowl.

In the bowl of a stand mixer fitted with the paddle attachment, beat the butter and the cream cheese until creamy. Add the granulated sugar and beat for at least 4 minutes, or until fluffy. Add the vanilla and the lemon zest and juice and beat until incorporated. Add the eggs, one at a time, and beat until incorporated. Add the flour mixture in three additions, alternating with the milk and beating after each addition. Transfer the batter to the prepared pan and bake for 50 to 55 minutes, or until a wooden pick inserted in the centre comes out clean. Place the pan on a rack and let the cake cool completely at room temperature then invert the cake onto the rack.

For the glaze, place the icing sugar in a medium bowl. While stirring constantly, gradually add the lemon juice, bit by bit, until the glaze is thick but pourable. Pour the glaze over the cooled cake and let set at room temperature. The pound cake can be wrapped in plastic wrap and stored at room temperature for up to 3 days.

Biscotti morbidi alle mandorle

CHEWY ALMOND COOKIES

INGREDIENTS
Makes about 20 cookies

- 480 g (4 cups) almond flour
- 420 g (2 cups plus 4 teaspoons) granulated sugar
- 5 large organic egg whites
- ¼ teaspoon fine salt
- 1 teaspoon pure vanilla extract or paste (or the seeds of 1 vanilla bean pod)
- 1 teaspoon pure almond oil or extract
- 80 g (⅔ cup) icing sugar for coating

Every time, almond is used in a recipe, I smile of joy! And this recipe will make you smile too (if you like almonds, that is). Simple, easy to make, and full of flavour! A perfect recipe for afternoon tea!

METHOD Preheat the oven to 170°C (335°F). Line a baking sheet with parchment paper.

Sift the almond flour into a large bowl. Add 300 g (1½ cups) of the granulated sugar and stir to combine.

In the bowl of a stand mixer fitted with the whisk attachment, whip the egg whites and salt until stiff peaks form. Add half of the almond flour mixture and use a spatula to gently fold it into the egg whites. Add the vanilla and almond extract and fold until incorporated. Add the remaining almond flour mixture and gently fold to combine.

Place the remaining granulated sugar on a plate. Place the icing sugar on a plate.

Using a spoon or an ice cream scoop, scoop up balls of dough. Roll the balls in the granulated sugar then toss them in the icing sugar. Place the balls of dough on the prepared baking sheet and use your hands to lightly press each cookie into the baking sheet. The balls should stay quite round. Bake for about 20 minutes, or until very lightly golden. Place the baking sheet on a rack and let the cookies cool before serving. These cookies can be stored in an airtight container at room temperature for up to 5 days.

Biscotti allo zafferano e limone senza uova

EGG-FREE SAFFRON AND LEMON COOKIES

INGREDIENTS

Makes about 20 cookies

- ½ teaspoon saffron strands
- 4 teaspoons whole milk, warm, plus more as needed
- Zest of 2 organic lemons
- 1 teaspoon pure lemon extract or oil
- 200 g (¾ cup plus 2 tablespoons) unsalted butter, at room temperature
- 200 g (1 cup) granulated sugar
- 400 g (2¾ cups plus 2 tablespoons) plain flour (all-purpose flour)

NOTE I use a round cookie cutter to make these cookies, but you can use any shape you desire.

I discovered saffron in desserts while traveling in Sri Lanka a very long time ago. I always thought the golden spice was only meant for savoury dishes, but it makes a surprisingly luxurious addition to cakes and other desserts. This recipe is primarily dedicated to those who are allergic to or intolerant of eggs, but please feel free to make a vegan or gluten-free version. Simply swap the equivalent ingredients and the results will be just as delicious. Using plant-based milk may deliver a slightly different flavour, but it will still be very special. The lemon zest lends a fresh note, while the butter gives these cookies their rich texture.

METHOD Preheat the oven to 170°C (335°F). Line two baking sheets with parchment paper.

In a small cup, combine the saffron strands and warm milk and stir until the saffron is completely dissolved, providing that distinctive gold colour. Add the lemon zest and lemon extract and stir to combine.

In the bowl of a stand mixer fitted with the paddle attachment, beat the butter and granulated sugar until pale and fluffy. Add the saffron mixture and beat until fully combined. Add the plain flour and mix on low until a dough forms. If the dough isn't coming together, add a few drops of milk and mix to incorporate. On a lightly floured work surface, use a rolling pin to roll out the dough until about 6 mm (¼ inch) thick. Using a medium round cookie cutter, cut the dough into shapes and place the cookies on the prepared baking sheet. Bake for about 15 minutes, or until firm but still light in colour. Place the baking sheet on a rack and let the cookies cool completely before serving. These cookies can be stored in an airtight container at room temperature for about 5 days.

Torta vaniglia e fragole

VANILLA AND STRAWBERRY LAYER CAKE

INGREDIENTS
Makes 1 (20 cm / 8 inch) cake
Makes about 10 servings

For the cake
- 300 ml (1¼ cups) whole milk, at room temperature
- 4 large organic eggs, at room temperature
- 2½ tablespoons vegetable oil, preferably non-GMO
- 1½ teaspoons pure vanilla extract or paste or the seeds of 1½ vanilla bean pods
- Zest of 1 organic lemon
- 400 g (2¾ cups plus 2 tablespoons) gluten-free pastry flour
- 350 g (1¾ cups) granulated sugar
- 2 teaspoons baking powder
- 1 teaspoons baking soda
- ½ teaspoon fine salt
- 180 g (¾ cup plus 1 tablespoon) unsalted butter, at room temperature and cut into small pieces

For the frosting
- 500 ml (2 cups plus 1 tablespoon) double whipping cream (heavy cream)
- 100 g (¾ cup plus 1 tablespoon) icing sugar (confectioners' sugar)
- 1 teaspoon pure vanilla extract or paste (or the seeds of 1 vanilla bean pod)
- 300 g (10½ ounces) strawberries, chopped and mashed

NOTE It's important to use the frosting right away, so wait to make it until you are ready to assemble the cake.

This layer cake is a classic you must have in your repertoire. And you can make it whatever you wish—a birthday cake, a celebration cake, a Saint Valentine cake, or even a Christmas Cake if you omit the strawberries and add orange zest and a few drops of amaretto to the sponge. Play around with different flavours, but stick to this super easy method, and you will end up with countless enjoyable variations.

METHOD For the cake, preheat the oven to 170°C (335°F). Grease two 20 cm (8 inch) shallow round cake pans then line the bottoms with parchment paper.

In a medium jug or bowl, whisk together the milk, eggs, and vegetable oil. Add the vanilla and lemon zest.

Sift the pastry flour into the bowl of a stand mixer fitted with the paddle attachment. Add the granulated sugar, baking powder, baking soda, and salt. With the mixer on low, gradually add the butter, piece by piece, and beat until fully incorporated. Add the milk mixture in three additions and beat on low until fully combined. Continue beating until the batter is pale and smooth. Scrape down the bowl then divide the batter between the prepared pans. Bake for 35 to 40 minutes, or until a wooden pick inserted in the centre of each cake comes out clean. Set the pans on a rack and let the cakes cool for about 15 minutes then invert the cakes onto the rack and let cool completely at room temperature.

For the frosting, in the bowl of a stand mixer fitted with the whisk attachment, whip the double whipping cream until medium-stiff peaks form. Add the icing sugar then add the vanilla and whip until stiff peaks form, being careful not to overwhip the cream. Add the mashed strawberries and use a rubber spatula to gently combine.

Use a serrated knife to trim just the dark part on top of each cake layer. Place one cake layer on a cake stand or serving plate. Use a rubber spatula to spread the frosting evenly over the cake then place the second cake layer on top. Using an off-set spatula, frost the top and sides of the cake. Decorate as you please, adding frosting rosettes and fresh strawberries, or sprinkles, or white chocolate shavings or chips... Enjoy!

Depression Era Chocolate Cake

INGREDIENTS

Makes 1 (20 cm / 8 inch) cake
Makes about 12 servings

For the cake

- 400 g (2¾ cups plus 2 tablespoons) plain flour (all-purpose flour)
- 420 g (2 cups plus 4 teaspoons) granulated sugar
- 60 g (¾ cup) unsweetened cocoa powder
- 2 teaspoons baking powder
- 2 teaspoons baking soda
- ½ teaspoon fine salt
- 3 tablespoons white wine vinegar or apple cider vinegar
- 180 ml (¾ cup) vegetable oil, preferably non-GMO
- 2 teaspoons pure vanilla extract or paste (or the seeds of 2 vanilla bean pods)
- 475 ml (2 cups) freshly brewed coffee, hot

For the frosting

- 2 tablespoons vegan butter
- 115 g (⅓ cup plus 2 tablespoons plus 1 teaspoon) spreadable vegan cream cheese, at room temperature
- 1 teaspoon pure vanilla extract or paste (or the seeds of 1 vanilla bean pod)
- 250 g (2 cups plus 1 tablespoon) vegan icing sugar (confectioners' sugar)
- 60 g (¾ cup) unsweetened cocoa powder

NOTE You can leave this cake unfrosted and simply dust some icing sugar over it, or you can melt some dark chocolate and pour it all over the top. You can use the same amount of light brown sugar in place of the granulated sugar.

As you might have noticed, I have not translated the title of this recipe. This cake isn't part of my Italian heritage; it comes from America and has a very interesting backstory. During the Great Depression (1929–1939), ingredients like milk, eggs, and butter were very scarce and very expensive. The U.S. Government issued "War Economy in Food" pamphlets to inform people of the importance of saving and reducing the consumption of certain foods. Because "necessity is the mother of invention", American cooks created new recipes omitting and replacing ingredients. This cake is one of those recipes, and it continues to be very popular today. I don't mean to sound catastrophic, but seeing how the world is unfolding, I wonder if we will have to face another period like that very soon… I keep this extremely easy recipe on hand, just in case. You never know…

METHOD For the cake, preheat the oven to 165°C (325°F). Grease two 20 cm (8 inch) round cake pans then line the bottoms with parchment paper.

In a large bowl, whisk together the plain flour, granulated sugar, cocoa powder, baking powder, baking soda, and salt. Create a well in the middle and pour in the white wine vinegar, vegetable oil, and vanilla. Pour the hot coffee over the entire mixture and whisk until the coffee is fully incorporated and the batter is smooth with no air bubbles. Divide the batter between the prepared pans and bake for 45 to 50 minutes, or until a wooden pick inserted in the centre of each cake comes out clean. Place the pans on a rack and let the cakes cool for 10 minutes then invert the cakes onto the rack and let cool completely at room temperature.

For the frosting, in a small pan over low heat or in the microwave, slowly melt the butter then let it cool slightly.

In the bowl of a stand mixer fitted with the paddle attachment, beat the cream cheese and the melted and cooled butter until creamy. Add the vanilla, followed by the icing sugar and cocoa powder and mix on low until incorporated. Be careful to not overmix the frosting.

Place one cake layer on a cake board, or stand, or serving plate. Using a rubber spatula, spread some frosting on top. Place the second cake layer on top then use an off-set spatula to frost the top and sides of the cake. For creamier frosting, let the cake stand at room temperature until ready to serve. For firmer frosting, place it in the refrigerator. This cake can be stored in the refrigerator for up to 3 days.

Victoria Sponge

INGREDIENTS

Makes 1 (20 cm / 8 inch) cake
Makes about 8 servings

For the cake

· 455 ml (1¾ cups plus 2½ tablespoons) almond milk or other plant-based milk
· 160 ml (⅔ cup) vegetable oil, preferably non-GMO
· 1 tablespoon apple cider vinegar
· 2 teaspoons pure vanilla extract or paste (or the seeds of 2 vanilla bean pods)
· 500 g (3½ cups plus 1 tablespoon) plain flour (all-purpose flour)
· 300 g (1½ cups) granulated sugar
· 2 teaspoons baking powder
· Pinch of fine salt

For the frosting

· 130 g (½ cup plus 1 tablespoon) unsalted vegan butter
· 260 g (2 cups plus 2 tablespoons) icing sugar (confectioners' sugar), plus more for dusting
· 1 teaspoon pure vanilla extract or paste (or the seeds of 1 vanilla bean pod)

For the filling

· 190 g (½ cup) good quality strawberry jam

I've noticed that vegan home bakers learning new recipes often feel overwhelmed by all the ingredient substitutions required. Strangely named or never heard of before ingredients can scare people away! My wish is to provide newbie vegan bakers, as well as more experienced ones, with some basic and easy alternatives to classic recipes. I encourage you to keep it simple, but with a good base recipe, you can make lots of variations.

Victoria sponge is a British classic—no afternoon tea in Britain can be called as such if a slice of this cake isn't on the table. Vegan whipping cream can be hard to find, though specialty shops surely have it. The vegetarian options have milk protein added, so they're not suitable for vegans. If you can find vegan whipping cream where you live, you can definitely whip it up and use it to fill your cake—it will likely give the cake a lighter texture and flavour. And if you don't want any cream at all, just use strawberry jam and dust some icing sugar over the cake. I am absolutely sure it will be a success!

METHOD For the cake, preheat the oven to 170°C (335°F). Grease two 20 cm (8 inch) round cake pans then line the bottoms with parchment paper. Fit a piping bag with the pastry tip of your choice (or simply cut the tip after you add the frosting).

In a large jug or bowl, whisk together the almond milk, vegetable oil, apple cider vinegar, and vanilla.

Sift the plain flour into a large bowl. Add the granulated sugar, baking powder, and salt and whisk to combine. Make a well in the centre and slowly add the almond milk mixture, whisking until smooth. Divide the batter between the prepared pans and bake for 35 to 40 minutes, or until a wooden pick inserted in the centre of each cake comes out clean. Place the pans on a rack and let the cakes cool for 5 minutes then invert the cakes onto the rack and let cool completely at room temperature.

For the frosting, in the bowl of a stand mixer fitted with the paddle attachment, or in a large bowl with an electric mixer, beat the butter until creamy. With the mixer on low, gradually add the icing sugar, bit by bit, and beat until fully incorporated. Add the vanilla and beat until light and fluffy. Transfer the frosting to the prepared piping bag, cutting the tip if necessary.

Place one cake layer on a serving plate or cake stand. If the cake has a dome on top, use a serrated knife to make the surface flat. Use an off-set spatula to spread a layer of jam evenly on top. Pipe the frosting in a nice pattern over the jam. Place the second cake layer on top. Dust the cake with icing sugar before serving. This cake can be kept in an airtight container at room temperature for up to 2 days.

Loaf al limone verde e cocco

LIME AND COCONUT LOAF

METHOD For the loaf, preheat the oven to 170°C (335°F). Grease a 24 x 14 cm (9½ x 5½ inch) loaf pan then line it with parchment paper. Set a rack inside a baking sheet.

Sift the pastry flour into a large bowl. Add the baking powder and whisk to combine.

In the bowl of stand mixer fitted with the paddle attachment, beat the butter and granulated sugar until pale and fluffy. Add the lime zest and the vanilla and beat to combine.

In a small bowl, briefly whisk the eggs. With the mixer on low, gradually add the beaten eggs in a steady stream and mix until incorporated. Add the flour mixture and use a rubber spatula to fold it into the batter. Add the coconut milk and stir to incorporate. Pour the batter into the prepared pan and bake for about 50 minutes, or until a wooden pick inserted in the centre comes out clean. Place the pan on the rack set in the baking sheet and let the loaf cool slightly then remove the loaf from the pan, set it on the rack, and let it cool completely at room temperature.

For the drizzle, in a small saucepan over low heat, combine the granulated sugar and lime juice and cook, stirring occasionally, until the sugar is completely melted and the liquid has a dense yet pourable consistency. Remove from the heat and let cool slightly.

When the drizzle has cooled, pour it all over the loaf and leave it to soak while the loaf is cooling.

Dust with icing sugar. This loaf can be stored in an airtight container at room temperature for up to 3 days.

INGREDIENTS

**Makes 1 loaf
(24 x 14 cm / 9½ x 5½ inch)**

For the loaf
· 230 g (1⅔ cups)
  gluten-free pastry flour
· 1½ teaspoons baking
  powder
· 226 g (1 cup) unsalted
  butter, at room temperature
· 230 g (1 cup plus
  2 tablespoons)
  granulated sugar
· Zest of 3 organic limes
· 1 teaspoon pure vanilla
  extract or paste (or the
  seeds of 1 vanilla bean pod)
· 4 large organic eggs
· 60 ml (¼ cup) full-fat
  coconut milk,
  at room temperature

For the drizzle
· About 65 g (⅓ cup)
  granulated sugar
· 70 ml (¼ cup plus 2
  teaspoons) freshly
  squeezed organic lime juice

For decoration
· Icing sugar (confectioners'
  sugar), for dusting

If this loaf could speak, it would say, "Make me! Make me! Make me!!!" No matter the occasion, if the sun is up and warm, this loaf cake screams, "Picnic! Party! Summer!" You can even bring it to the beach for a quick snack for you and your kids. In Italy, limes are mostly available in the summer, but this cake freezes really well, so I like to bake it while limes are still in season then freeze it and defrost it during autumn, when the days are shorter and the rain comes down. A nice cup of tea and a slice of this cake are all I need to focus on new projects and brighten even the darkest afternoon.

Quadrati al limone

LEMON SQUARES

INGREDIENTS
Serves about 16 squares

For the base crust
- 125 g (¾ cup plus 2 tablespoons) gluten-free pastry flour
- 60 g (½ cup) almond flour
- 60 g (½ cup) icing sugar (confectioners' sugar), plus more for dusting
- Pinch of fine salt
- 110 g (7 tablespoons plus 2 teaspoons) unsalted butter, cold and cut into small pieces

For the filling
- 215 g (1 cup plus 1 tablespoon) granulated sugar
- 3 large organic eggs plus 3 large organic egg yolks, at room temperature
- Pinch of fine salt
- Zest of 3 organic lemons
- 240 g (8½ ounces) freshly squeezed organic lemon juice
- 60 g (¼ cup plus 1 teaspoon) unsalted butter, room temperature
- 40 g (1½ ounces) double whipping cream (heavy cream)

I won't say much this time, because I reckon there is no need to convince you to make these lemon squares. You don't need a gluten allergy or intolerance to enjoy these beautiful bars. They are super tangy, super fresh, and super cute! Well, if you don't like lemons, these definitely are not for you, but can someone not like lemon in desserts?

METHOD For the crust, preheat the oven to 170°C (335°F). Grease a 20 cm (8 inch) square cake pan then line it with parchment paper, leaving some hanging over the sides.

In a large bowl, whisk together the pastry flour, almond flour, icing sugar, and salt. Add the butter and use your fingers to rub it into the flour mixture until sandy and crumbly. Press the mixture evenly into the bottom of the prepared pan and bake for 15 to 17 minutes, or until golden. Place the pan on a rack and let the crust cool. Leave the oven on.

For the filling, in a medium saucepan, combine the granulated sugar, whole eggs, eggs yolks, and salt. Quickly but gently whisk to combine without making the eggs frothy. Add the lemon zest and juice and whisk to combine. Place the pan over medium heat, add the butter, and cook, stirring constantly, until the curd is thick and leaves a film on the back of a wooden spoon. Be careful to keep the mixture from boiling or you will cook the eggs. Pour the curd through a fine-mesh sieve set over a bowl. Add the double whipping cream and stir to fully incorporate. Pour the mixture over the prebaked crust and bake for 15 minutes, or until the filling is set but still jiggles a little in the centre. Place the pan on a rack and let the bars cool completely then refrigerate for at least 2 hours and preferably overnight. When ready to serve, use the parchment paper to lift the bars out of the pan then use a long, sharp knife to cut them into squares. Serve right away. These lemon bars can be stored in an airtight container in the refrigerator for up to 4 days.

Torta alle pere e cioccolato

PEAR AND CHOCOLATE CAKE

INGREDIENTS

· 325 g (1¼ cups plus
  3 tablespoons) unsalted
  butter, at room temperature
· 320 g (1½ cups plus
  4 teaspoons) light brown
  sugar, plus more for dusting
· 2 teaspoons pure vanilla
  extract or paste
  (or the seeds of
  2 vanilla bean pods)
· 5 large organic eggs
· 320 g (2⅔ cups)
  almond flour
· 60 g (6 tablespoons)
  gluten-free pastry flour
· ½ teaspoon ground
  cinnamon
· 3 pears, peeled, cored,
  and sliced
· 120 g (4¼ ounces) dark
  chocolate, roughly chopped

It's no secret that I love rustic cakes more than anything. To me, they are romantic, warm, wholesome, and real! While many believe they are easy to make—perhaps that's true—I have seen plenty of pastry chefs fail at making them. With a rustic cake, one needs to know what one is doing, of course, but most of all, one must feel the cake, love the process, and really get in touch with the ingredients and texture. Rustic cakes are made with the soul and not with technique. And this is why I love rustic cakes. This one combines pear and chocolate, a very popular combination in Italy. I like to use Bosc pears, but any variety will work.

METHOD Preheat the oven to 170°C (335°F). Line the base and the sides of a 23 cm (9 inch) springform pan with parchment paper.

In the bowl of a stand mixer fitted with the paddle attachment, beat the butter and brown sugar until fluffy. Add the vanilla. Add the eggs, one at a time, and beat well after each addition. With the mixer on low, add the almond flour, pastry flour, and cinnamon and mix until combined. Pour half of the batter into the prepared pan. Place half of the sliced pears on top then sprinkle with half of the chocolate. Pour the rest of the batter on top, spreading it evenly, and bake for 15 to 20 minutes. Remove the cake from the oven but leave the oven on. Sprinkle the cake with the remaining chopped chocolate and top with the remaining pear slices. Sprinkle with a little brown sugar and bake for 18 to 20 minutes, or until a wooden pick inserted in the centre comes out clean. Place the pan on a rack and the cake cool slightly then release and remove the sides of the pan. This cake is wonderful slightly warm! This cake can be stored in an airtight container at room temperature for up to 3 days.

Torta alle banane e crema al formaggio

BANANA AND CREAM CHEESECAKE

INGREDIENTS

**Makes 1 cake
(21.5 cm / 8½ inch)**

For the cake

· 300 g (2 cups plus
  2 tablespoons) gluten-free
  pastry flour
· 2 teaspoons baking powder
· 1 teaspoon baking soda
· Pinch of fine salt
· 3 ripe bananas
· 115 ml (¼ cup plus 3
  tablespoons) vegetable oil,
  preferably non-GMO
· 300 g (1½ cups)
  granulated sugar
· 3 large organic eggs
· Zest and juice
  of 1 organic lemon
· 2 teaspoons pure vanilla
  extract or paste (or the
  seeds of 2 vanilla bean pod)

For the cream cheese frosting

· 113 (½ cup) unsalted butter,
  at room temperature
· 250 g (1 cup plus
  2 teaspoons) full-fat
  spreadable cream cheese
· 1 teaspoon pure vanilla
  extract or paste (or the
  seeds of 1 vanilla bean pod)
· 450 g (3¾ cups) icing sugar
  (confectioners' sugar)

For decorating

· Poppy seeds (optional)

Banana, like coconut, is one of those ingredients many people don't like. I happen to love banana—and coconut—and whenever I can, I bake banana bread or banana cake. In the United States, banana cakes are very popular and often made for school bake sales. I don't recall bake sales at school when I was growing up in Italy. It's not one of our traditions, but why not start a new one? Whether for a bake sale, or simply a lazy afternoon at home, this cake is tender, moist, and full of flavour. It never disappoints—even if it is gluten free.

METHOD For the cake, preheat the oven to 170°C (335°F). Grease a 21.5 cm (8½ inch) square cake pan or a 21.5 x 33 cm (8½ x 13 inch) rectangular cake pan then line the bottom with parchment.

In a large bowl, whisk together the pastry flour, baking powder, baking soda, and salt.

Peel, cut, and mash the bananas then place them in a medium bowl.

In a large bowl, whisk together the vegetable oil, granulated sugar, eggs, lemon zest and juice, and vanilla. Add the mashed bananas and stir to fully combine. Add the flour mixture and stir until fully incorporated. Pour the batter into the prepared pan and bake for 30 to 35 minutes, or until a wooden pick inserted in the centre comes out clean. Place the pan on the rack and let the cake cool completely.

For the cream cheese frosting, in the bowl of a stand mixer fitted with the paddle attachment, beat the butter until creamy. Add the cream cheese and beat until smooth, being careful to not overbeat the mixture or the frosting will lose its texture. Stir in the vanilla. With the mixer on low, gradually add the icing sugar, bit by bit, then beat on high for few seconds.

When the cake is completely cool, invert it onto a serving plate. Spread the frosting evenly over the top, moving an offset spatula up and down to create waves in the frosting. Finish with some poppy seeds to decorate then cut into squares and serve.

Biscotti rugosi al cioccolato

CHOCOLATE CRINKLE COOKIES

INGREDIENTS

- 113 g (½ cup) unsalted butter, at room temperature
- 200 g (1 cup) granulated sugar
- 220 g (1 cup plus 4 teaspoons) light or dark brown sugar
- 4 large organic eggs
- 2 teaspoons pure vanilla extract or paste (or the seeds of 2 vanilla bean pods
- 280 g (2 cups) gluten-free pastry flour
- 90 g (1 cup plus 2 tablespoons) unsweetened cocoa powder
- 1 teaspoon baking powder
- 1 teaspoon baking soda
- 1 teaspoon ground coffee
- Pinch of fine salt
- 300 g (1⅔ cups) mini chocolate chips

For finishing

- 250 g (2 cups plus 1 tablespoon) icing sugar (confectioners' sugar)
- 100 g (½ cup) granulated sugar

The future looks bright if a recipe like this is around. Cookies are loved, pretty much universally, and chocolate cookies are always a win! These cookies are not at all dry. On the contrary, they are chewy and this is what I like about them. Make them for the holidays, but not only at the holidays. Actually, make them whenever you want, and do yourself a favour—dunk them in a glass of cold plant-based milk! Enjoy... you can thank me later...

METHOD In the bowl of a stand mixer fitted with the paddle attachment, or in a large bowl if using an electric mixer, beat the butter, granulated sugar, and brown sugar until creamy. Add the eggs, one at a time, then add the vanilla and beat until incorporated. With the mixer on low, start adding the pastry flour, cocoa powder, baking powder, baking soda, ground coffee, and salt and beat until incorporated. Add the mini chocolate chips and use a rubber spatula to fold the chips in by hand. Gather the dough, wrap it in plastic wrap, and refrigerate overnight.

When the dough has chilled, preheat the oven to 170°C (335°F). Line two baking sheets with parchment paper.

In a small, shallow bowl, whisk together the icing sugar and granulated sugar for finishing.

Using an ice cream scoop or a normal spoon, scoop pieces of dough measuring about 1½ tablespoons each and roll them into a ball. Roll each ball in the sugar mixture and place on the prepared baking sheet, leaving some space for the cookies to expand. Bake for 10 to 12 minutes, or until crunchy around the edges but a little soft in the middle. When the cookies are baked, use a round cookie cutter (or a glass) slightly larger than the cookies to scoot each cookie around and make it into a perfect circle. Place the baking sheets on racks and let the cookies cool completely before serving.

INDEX

DESIGN AND LAYOUT
Isabella Mancioli

CREATIVE PRODUCER
Chiara Panetti

PHOTO ASSISTANTS
Martina D'Andrea
Melania Commodo
Giulia Gerosa

POST-PRODUCTION
Lorenzo Bataloni
Samuele Donnini

FOOD STYLIST
Giovanna Di Lisciandro

STYLIST
Emma Danieli

MAKE-UP AND HAIR STYLIST
Noemi Turrini

THANKS TO
Barbara Natalucci
Benedetta Canale

EDITORIAL DIRECTION
Claudia Schönecker

PROJECT MANAGEMENT
Veronika Brandt

COPYEDITING
Lauren Salkeld

PRODUCTION MANAGEMENT
Luisa Klose

SEPARATIONS
Reproline Mediateam

© Prestel Verlag,
Munich · London · New York, 2024

A member of Penguin Random House
Verlagsgruppe GmbH

Neumarkter Strasse 28 · 81673 Munich

© TEXT
Melissa Forti, 2024

© PHOTOGRAPHS
Giovanna Di Lisciandro, 2024

Library of Congress Control Number is available; a
CIP catalogue record for this book is available from
the British Library.

PRINTING AND BINDING
Livonia Print, Riga

Penguin Random House Verlagsgruppe
FSC® N001967

MIX
Paper | Supporting
responsible forestry
FSC® C002795

Printed in Latvia

ISBN 978-3-7913-8986-8

www.prestel.com